RECOVERING FRO

for

The Body
Keeps
The Score

BRAIN, MIND, AND BODY IN THE HEALING OF TRAUMA

BESSEL VAN DER KOLK, MD.

- Final Volume -

presented by

RODNEY CUNNINGHAM

CONTENT

PART 4:

THE IMPRINT OF TRAUMA

PART 5:

PATHS TO RECOVERY

EPILOGUE: CHOICES TO BE MADE

PART 5

PATHS TO RECOVERY

CHAPTER 18

FILLING IN THE HOLES: CREATING STRUCTURES

The greatest discovery of my generation is that human beings can alter their lives by altering their attitudes of mind.

—**William James**

It is not that something different is seen, but that one sees differently. It is as though the spatial act of seeing were changed by a new dimension.

—**Carl Jung**

I t is one thing to process memories of trauma, but it is an entirely different matter to confront the inner void—the holes in the soul that result from not having been wanted, not having been seen, and not having been allowed to speak the truth. If your parents' faces never lit up when they looked at you, it's hard to know what it feels like to be loved and cherished. If you come from an incomprehensible world filled with secrecy and fear, it's almost impossible to find the words to express what you have endured. If you grew up unwanted and ignored, it is a major challenge to develop a visceral sense of agency and self-worth.

The research that Judy Herman, Chris Perry, and I had done (see chapter 9) showed that people who felt unwanted as children, and those who did not remember feeling safe with anyone while growing up, did not fully benefit from conventional psychotherapy, presumably because they could not activate old traces of feeling cared for.

I could see this even in some of my most committed and articulate patients. Despite their hard work in therapy and their share of personal and professional accomplishments, they could not erase the devastating imprints of a mother who was too depressed to notice them or a father who treated them like he wished they'd never been born. It was clear that their lives would change fundamentally only if they could reconstruct those implicit maps. But how? How can we help people become viscerally acquainted with feelings that were lacking early in their lives?

I glimpsed a possible answer when I attended the founding conference of the United States Association for Body Psychotherapy in June 1994 at a small college in Beverley on the rocky Massachusetts coast. Ironically, I had been asked to represent mainstream psychiatry at the meeting and to speak on using brain scans to visualize mental states. But as soon as I walked into the lobby where attendees had gathered for morning coffee, I realized this was a different crowd from my usual psychopharmacology or psychotherapy gatherings. The way they talked to one another, their postures and gestures, radiated vitality and engagement—the sort of physical reciprocity that is the essence of attunement.

I soon struck up a conversation with Albert Pesso, a stocky former dancer with the Martha Graham Dance Company who was then in his early seventies. Underneath his bushy eyebrows he exuded kindness and confidence. He told me that he had found a way of fundamentally changing people's relationship to their core, somatic selves. His enthusiasm was infectious, but I was skeptical and asked him if he was certain he could change the settings of the amygdala. Unfazed by the fact that nobody had ever tested his method scientifically, he confidently assured me that he could.

Pesso was about to conduct a workshop in "PBSP psychomotor therapy,"[1] and he invited me to attend. It was unlike any group work I had ever seen. He took a low chair opposite a woman named Nancy, whom he called a "protagonist," with the other participants seated on pillows around them. He then invited Nancy to talk about what was troubling her, occasionally using her pauses to "witness" what he was observing—as in "A witness can see how crestfallen you are when you talk about your father deserting the family." I was impressed by how carefully he tracked subtle shifts in body posture, facial expression, tone of voice, and eye gaze, the nonverbal expressions of emotion. (This is called "microtracking" in psychomotor therapy).

Each time Pesso made a "witness statement," Nancy's face and body relaxed a bit, as if she felt comforted by being seen and validated. His quiet comments seemed to bolster her courage to continue and go deeper. When Nancy started to cry, he observed that nobody should have to bear so much pain all by herself, and he asked if she would like to choose someone to sit next to her. (He called this a "contact person.") Nancy nodded and, after carefully scanning the room, pointed to a kind-looking middle-aged woman. Pesso asked Nancy where she would like her contact person to sit. "Right here," Nancy said decisively, indicating a pillow immediately to her right.

I was fascinated. People process spatial relations with the right hemisphere of the brain, and our neuroimaging research had shown that the imprint of trauma is principally on the right hemisphere as well (see chapter 3). Caring, disapproval, and indifference all are primarily conveyed by facial expression, tone of voice, and physical movements. According to recent research, up to 90 percent of human communication occurs in the nonverbal, right-hemisphere realm,[2] and this was where Pesso's work seemed primarily to be directed. As the workshop went on, I was also struck by how the contact person's presence seemed to help Nancy tolerate the painful experiences she was dredging up.[3]

But what was most unusual was how Pesso created tableaus—or as he called them, "structures"—of the protagonists' past. As the narratives unfolded, group participants were asked to play the roles of significant people in the protagonists' lives, such as parents and other family members, so that their inner world began to take form in three-dimensional space. Group members were also enlisted to play the ideal, wished-for parents who would provide the support, love, and protection that had been lacking at critical moments. Protagonists became the directors of their own plays, creating around them the past they never had, and they clearly experienced profound physical and mental relief after these imaginary scenarios. Could this technique instill imprints of safety and comfort alongside those of terror and abandonment, decades after the original shaping of mind and brain?

Intrigued with the promise of Pesso's work, I eagerly accepted his invitation to visit his hilltop farmhouse in southern New Hampshire. After lunch beneath an ancient oak tree, Al asked me to join him in his red clapboard barn, now a studio, to do a structure. I'd spent several years in psychoanalysis, so I did not expect any major revelations. I was a settled professional man in my forties with my own family, and I thought of my parents as two elderly people who were trying to create a decent old age for themselves. I certainly did not think they still had a major influence on me.

Since there were no other people available for role-play, Al began by asking me to select an object or a piece of furniture to represent my father. I chose a gigantic black leather couch and asked Al to put it upright about eight feet in front of me, slightly to the left. Then he asked if I'd like to bring my mother into the room as well, and I chose a heavy lamp, approximately the same height as the upright couch. As the session continued, the space became populated with the important people in my life: my best friend, a tiny Kleenex box to my right; my wife, a small pillow next to him; my two children, two more tiny pillows.

After a while I surveyed the projection of my internal landscape: two hulking, dark, and threatening objects representing my parents and an array of minuscule objects representing my wife, children, and friends. I was astounded; I had re-created my inner image of my stern Calvinistic parents from the time I was a little boy. My chest felt tight, and I'm sure that my voice sounded even tighter. I could not deny what my spatial brain was revealing: The structure had allowed me to visualize my implicit map of the world.

When I told Al what I had just uncovered, he nodded and asked if I would allow him to change my perspective. I felt my skepticism return, but I liked Al and was curious about his method, so I hesitantly agreed. He then interposed his body directly between me and the couch and lamp, making them disappear from my line of sight. Instantaneously I felt a deep release in my body—the constriction in my chest eased and my breathing became relaxed. That was the moment I decided to become Pesso's student.[4]

RESTRUCTURING INNER MAPS

Projecting your inner world into the three-dimensional space of a structure enables you to see what's happening in the theater of your mind and gives you a much clearer perspective on your reactions to people and events in the past. As you position placeholders for the important people in your life, you may be surprised by the unexpected memories, thoughts, and emotions that come up. You then can experiment with moving the pieces around on the external chessboard that you've created and see what effect it has on you.

Although the structures involve dialogue, psychomotor therapy does not explain or interpret the past. Instead, it allows you to feel what you felt back then, to visualize what you saw, and to say what you could not say when it actually happened. It's as if you could go back into the movie of your life and rewrite the crucial scenes. You can direct the role-players to do things they failed to do in the past, such as keeping your father from beating up your mom. These tableaus can stimulate powerful emotions. For example, as you place your "real mother" in the corner, cowering in terror, you may feel a deep longing to protect her and realize how powerless you felt as a child. But if you then create an ideal mother, who stands up to your father and who knows how to avoid getting trapped in abusive relationships, you may experience a visceral sense of relief and an unburdening of that old guilt and helplessness. Or you might confront the brother who brutalized you as a child and then create an ideal brother who protects you and becomes your role model.

The job of the director/therapist and other group members is to provide protagonists with the support they need to delve into whatever they have been too afraid to explore on their own. The safety of the group allows you to notice things that you have hidden from yourself—usually the things you are most ashamed of. When you no longer have to hide, the structure allows you to place the shame where it belongs—on the figures right in front of you who represent those who hurt you and made you feel helpless as a child.

Feeling safe means you can say things to your father (or, rather, the placeholder who represents him) that you wish you could have said as a five-year-old. You can tell the placeholder for your depressed and frightened mother how terrible you felt about not being able to take care of her. You can experiment with distance and proximity and explore what happens as you move placeholders around. As an active participant, you can lose yourself in a scene in a way you cannot when you simply tell a story. And as you take charge of representing the reality of your experience, the witness keeps you company, reflecting the changes in your posture, facial expression, and tone of voice.

In my experience, physically reexperiencing the past in the present and then reworking it in a safe and supportive "container" can be powerful enough to create new, supplemental memories: simulated experiences of growing up in an attuned, affectionate setting where you are protected from harm. Structures do not erase bad memories, or even neutralize them the way EMDR does. Instead, a structure offers fresh options—an alternative memory in which your basic human needs are met and your longings for love and protection are fulfilled.

REVISING THE PAST

Let me give an example from a workshop I led not long ago at the Esalen

Institute in Big Sur, California.

Maria was a slender, athletic Filipina in her midforties who had been pleasant and accommodating during our first two days, which had been devoted to exploring the long-term impact of trauma and teaching self-regulation techniques. But now, seated on her pillow about six feet away from me, she looked scared and collapsed. I wondered to myself if she had volunteered as a protagonist mainly to please the girlfriend who had accompanied her to the workshop.

I began by encouraging her to notice what was going on inside her and to share whatever came to mind. After a long silence she said: "I can't really feel anything in my body, and my mind is blank." Mirroring her inner tension, I replied: "A witness can see how worried you are that your mind is blank and you don't feel anything after volunteering to do a structure. Is that right?" "Yes!" she answered, sounding slightly relieved.

The "witness figure" enters the structure at the very beginning and takes the role of an accepting, nonjudgmental observer who joins the protagonist by reflecting his or her emotional state and noting the context in which that state has emerged (as when I mentioned Maria's "volunteering to do a structure"). Being validated by feeling heard and seen is a precondition for feeling safe, which is critical when we explore the dangerous territory of trauma and abandonment. A neuroimaging study has shown that when people hear a statement that mirrors their inner state, the right amygdala momentarily lights up, as if to underline the accuracy of the reflection.

I encouraged Maria to keep focusing on her breath, one of the exercises we had been practicing together, and to notice what she was feeling in her body. After another long silence she hesitantly began to speak: "There is always a sense of fear in everything I do. It doesn't look like I am afraid, but I am always pushing myself. It is really difficult for me to be up here." I reflected, "A witness can see how uncomfortable you feel pushing yourself to be here," and she nodded, slightly straightening her spine, signaling that she felt understood. She continued: "I grew up thinking that my family was normal. But I always was terrified of my dad. I never felt cared for by him. He never hit me as hard as he did my siblings, but I have a pervasive sense of fear." I noted that a witness could see how afraid she looked as she spoke of her father, and then I invited her to select a group member to represent him.

Maria scanned the room and chose Scott, a gentle video producer who had been a lively and supportive member of the group. I gave Scott his script: "I enroll as your real father, who terrified you when you were a little girl," which he repeated. (Note that this work is not about improvisation but about accurately enacting the dialogue and directions provided by the witness and protagonist.) I then asked Maria where she would like her real father to be positioned, and she instructed Scott to stand about twelve feet away, slightly to her right and facing away from her. We were beginning to create the tableau, and every time I conduct a structure I'm impressed by how precise the outward projections of the right hemisphere are. Protagonists always know exactly where the various characters in their structures should be located.

It also surprises me, again and again, how the placeholders representing the significant people in the protagonist's past almost immediately assume a virtual reality: The people who enroll seem to *become* the people he or she had to deal with back then—not only to the protagonist but often to the other participants as well. I encouraged Maria to take a good, long look at her real father, and as she gazed at him standing there, we could witness how her emotions shifted between terror and a deep sense of compassion for him. She tearfully reflected on how difficult his life had been—how, as a child during World War II, he had seen people beheaded; how he had been forced to eat rotten fish infested with maggots. Structures promote one of the essential conditions for deep therapeutic change: a trancelike state in which multiple realities can live side by side—past and present, knowing that you're an adult while feeling the way you did as a child, expressing your rage or terror to someone who feels like your abuser while being fully aware that you are talking to Scott, who is nothing like your real father, and experiencing simultaneously the complex emotions of loyalty, tenderness, rage, and longing that kids feel with their parents.

As Maria began to speak about their relationship when she was a little girl, I continued to mirror her expressions. Her father had brutalized her mother, she said. He was relentlessly critical of her diet, her body, her housekeeping, and she was always afraid for her mother when he berated her. Maria described her mother as loving and warm; she could not have survived without her. She would always be there to comfort Maria after her father lashed out at her, but she didn't do anything to protect her children from their father's rage. "I think my mom had a lot of fear herself. I have a sense that she didn't protect us because she felt trapped."

At this point I suggested that it was time to call Maria's real mother into the room. Maria scanned the group and smiled brightly as she asked Kristin, a blonde, Scandinavian-looking artist, to play the part of her real mother. Kristin accepted in the formal words of the structure: "I enroll as your real mother, who was warm and loving and without whom you would not have survived but who failed to protect you from your abusive father." Maria had her sit on a pillow to her right, much closer than her real father.

I encouraged Maria to look at Kristin and then I asked, "So what happens when you look at her?" Maria angrily said, "Nothing." "A witness would see how you stiffen as you look at your real mom and angrily say that you feel nothing," I noted. After a long silence I asked again, "So what happens now?" Maria looked slightly more collapsed and repeated, "Nothing." I asked her, "Is there something you want to say to your mom?" Finally Maria said, "I know you did the best you could," and then, moments later: "I wanted you to protect me." When she began to cry softly, I asked her, "What is happening inside?" "Holding my chest, my heart feels like it is pounding really hard," Maria said. "My sadness goes out to my mom; how incapable she was of standing up to my father and protecting us. She just shuts down, pretending everything's okay, and in her mind it probably is, and that makes me mad today. I want to say to her: 'Mom, when I see you react to dad when he is being mean . . . when I see your face, you look disgusted and I don't know why you don't say, "Fuck off." You don't know how to fight—you are such a pushover—there is a part of you that is not good and not alive. I don't even know what I want you to say. I just want you to be different—nothing you do is right, like you accept everything when it is totally not okay.'" I noted, "A witness would see how fierce you are as you want your mother to stand up to your dad." Maria then talked about how she wanted her mother to run off with the kids and take them away from her terrifying father.

I then suggested enrolling another group member to represent her ideal mother. Maria scanned the room again and chose Ellen, a therapist and martial artist. Maria placed her on a pillow to her right between her real mother and herself and asked Ellen to put her arm around her. "What do you want your ideal mother to say to your dad?" I asked. "I want her to say, 'If you are going to talk like that, I am going to leave you and take the kids,'" she answered. "'We are not going to sit here and listen to this shit.'" Ellen repeated Maria's words. Then I asked: "What happens now?" Maria responded: "I like it. I have a little pressure in my head. My breath is free. I have a subtle energetic dance in my body now. Sweet." "A witness can see how delighted you are when you hear your mother saying that she is not taking this shit from your dad anymore and that she will take you away from him," I told her. Maria began to sob and said, "I would have been able to be a safe, happy little girl." Out of the corner of my eye I could see several group members weeping silently—the possibility of growing up safe and happy clearly resonated with their own longings.

After a while I suggested that it was time to summon Maria's ideal father. I could clearly see the delight in Maria's eyes as she scanned the group, imagining her ideal father. She finally chose Danny. I gave him his script, and he gently told her: "I enroll as your ideal father, who would have loved you and cared for you and who would not have terrified you." Maria instructed him to take a seat near her on her left and beamed. "My healthy mom and dad!" she exclaimed. I responded: "Allow yourself to feel that joy as you look at an ideal dad who would have cared for you." Maria cried, "It's beautiful," and threw her arms around Danny, smiling at him through her tears. "I am remembering a really tender moment with my dad, and that is what this feels like. I would love to have my mom next to me too." Both ideal parents tenderly responded and cradled her. I left them there for a while so that they could fully internalize the experience.

We finished with Danny saying: "If I had been your ideal dad back then, I would have loved you just like this and not have inflicted my cruelty," while Ellen added, "If I had been your ideal mom, I would have stood up for you and me and protected you and not let any harm come to you." All the characters then made final statements, deenrolling from the roles they had played, and formally resumed being themselves.

RESCRIPTING YOUR LIFE

Nobody grows up under ideal circumstances—as if we even know what ideal circumstances are. As my late friend David Servan-Schreiber once said: every life is difficult in its own way. But we do know that, in order to become self-confident and capable adults, it helps enormously to have grown up with steady and predictable parents; parents who delighted in you, in your discoveries and explorations; parents who helped you organize your comings and goings; and who served as role models for self-care and getting along with other people.

Defects in any of these areas are likely to manifest themselves later in life. A child who has been ignored or chronically humiliated is likely to lack self-respect. Children who have not been allowed to assert themselves will probably have difficulty standing up for themselves as adults, and most grown-ups who were brutalized as children carry a smoldering rage that will take a great deal of energy to contain.

Our relationships will suffer as well. The more early pain and deprivation we have experienced, the more likely we are to interpret other people's actions as being directed against us and the less understanding we will be of their struggles, insecurities, and concerns. If we cannot appreciate the complexity of their lives, we may see anything they do as a confirmation that we are going to get hurt and disappointed.

In the chapters on the biology of trauma we saw how trauma and abandonment disconnect people from their body as a source of pleasure and comfort, or even as a part of themselves that needs care and nurturance. When we cannot rely on our body to signal safety or warning and instead feel chronically overwhelmed by physical stirrings, we lose the capacity to feel at home in our own skin and, by extension, in the world. As long as their map of the world is based on trauma, abuse, and neglect, people are likely to seek shortcuts to oblivion. Anticipating rejection, ridicule, and deprivation, they are reluctant to try out new options, certain that these will lead to failure. This lack of experimentation traps people in a matrix of fear, isolation, and scarcity where it is impossible to welcome the very experiences that might change their basic worldview.

This is one reason the highly structured experiences of psychomotor therapy are so valuable. Participants can safely project their inner reality into a space filled with real people, where they can explore the cacophony and confusion of the past. This leads to concrete aha moments: "Yes, that is what it was like. That is what I had to deal with. And that is what it would have felt like back then if I had been cherished and cradled." Acquiring a sensory experience of feeling treasured and protected as a three-year-old in the trancelike container of a structure allows people to rescript their inner experience, as in "I can spontaneously interact with other people without having to be afraid of being rejected or getting hurt."

Structures harness the extraordinary power of the imagination to transform the inner narratives that drive and confine our functioning in the world. With the proper support the secrets that once were too dangerous to be revealed can be disclosed not just to a therapist, a latter-day father confessor, but, in our imagination, to the people who actually hurt and betrayed us.

The three-dimensional nature of the structure transforms the hidden, the forbidden, and the feared into visible, concrete reality. In this it is somewhat similar to IFS, which we explored in the previous chapter. IFS calls forth the split-off parts that you created in order to survive and enables you to identify and talk with them, so that your undamaged Self can emerge. In contrast, a structure creates a three-dimensional image of whom and what you had to deal with and gives you a chance to create a different outcome.

Most people are hesitant to go into past pain and disappointment—it only promises to bring back the intolerable. But as they are mirrored and witnessed, a new reality begins to take shape. Accurate mirroring feels completely different from being ignored, criticized, and put down. It gives you permission to feel what you feel and know what you know—one of the essential foundations of recovery.

Trauma causes people to remain stuck in interpreting the present in light of an unchanging past. The scene you re-create in a structure may or may not be precisely what happened, but it represents the structure of your inner world: your internal map and the hidden rules that you have been living by.

DARING TO TELL THE TRUTH

I recently led another group structure with a twenty-six-year-old man named Mark, who at age thirteen had accidentally overheard his father having phone sex with his aunt, his mother's sister. Mark felt confused, embarrassed, hurt, betrayed, and paralyzed by this knowledge, but when he tried to talk with his father about it, he was met with rage and denial: he was told that he had a filthy imagination and accused of trying to break up the family. Mark never dared to tell his mom, but henceforth the family secrets and hypocrisy contaminated every aspect of his home life and gave him a pervasive sense that nobody could be trusted. After school, he spent his isolated adolescence hanging around neighborhood basketball courts or in his room watching TV. When he was twenty-one his mother died—of a broken heart, Mark says—and his father married the aunt. Mark was not invited to either the funeral or the wedding.

Secrets like these become inner toxins—realities that you are not allowed to acknowledge to yourself or to others but that nevertheless become the template of your life. I knew none of this history when Mark joined the group, but he stood out by his emotional distance, and during check-ins he acknowledged that he felt separated from everyone by a dense fog. I was quite worried about what would be revealed once we started to look behind his frozen, expressionless exterior.

When I invited Mark to talk about his family, he said a few words and then seemed to shut down even more. So I encouraged him to ask for a "contact figure" to support him. He chose a white-haired group member, Richard, and placed Richard on a pillow next to him, touching his shoulder. Then, as he began to tell his story, Mark placed Joe, as his real father, ten feet in front of him, and directed Carolyn, representing his mother, to crouch in a corner with her face hidden. Mark next asked Amanda to play his aunt, telling her to stand defiantly to one side, arms crossed over her chest—representing all the calculating, ruthless, and devious women who are after men.

Surveying the tableau he had created, Mark sat up straight, eyes wide open; clearly the fog had lifted. I said: "A witness can see how startled you are seeing what you had to deal with." Mark nodded appreciatively and remained silent and somber for some time. Then, looking at his "father," he burst out: "You asshole, you hypocrite, you ruined my life." I invited Mark to tell his "father" all the things that he had wanted to tell him but never could. A long list of accusations followed. I directed the "father" to respond physically as if he had been punched, so that Mark could see that that his blows had landed. It did not surprise me when Mark spontaneously said that he'd always worried that his rage would get out of control and that this fear had kept him from standing up for himself in school, at work, and in other relationships.

After Mark had confronted his "father," I asked if he would like Richard to assume a new role: that of his ideal father. I instructed Richard to look Mark directly in the eye and to say: "If I had been your ideal father back then, I would have listened to you and not accused you of having a filthy imagination." When Richard repeated this, Mark started to tremble. "Oh my God, life would have been so different if I could have trusted my father and talked about what was going on. I could have *had* a father." I then told Richard to say: "If I had been your ideal father back then, I would have welcomed your anger and you would have had a father you could have trusted." Mark visibly relaxed and said that would have made all the difference in the world.

Then Mark addressed the standin for his aunt. The group was visibly stunned as he unleashed a torrent of abuse on her: "You conniving whore, you backstabber. You betrayed your sister and ruined her life. You ruined our family." After he was done, Mark started to sob. He then said he'd always been deeply suspicious of any woman who showed an interest in him. The remainder of the structure took another half hour, in which we slowly set up conditions for him to create two new women: the ideal aunt, who did not betray her sister but who helped support their isolated immigrant family, and the ideal mother, who kept her husband's interest and devotion and so did not die of heartbreak. Mark ended the structure quietly surveying the scene he had created with a contented smile on his face.

For the remainder of the workshop Mark was an open and valuable member of the group, and three months later he sent me an e-mail saying that this experience had changed his life. He had recently moved in with his first girlfriend, and although they'd had some heated discussions about their new arrangement, he'd been able to take in her point of view without clamming up defensively, going back to his fear or rage, or feeling that she was trying to pull a fast one. He was amazed that he felt okay disagreeing with her and that he was able to stand up for himself. He then asked for the name of a therapist in his community to help with the huge changes he was making in his life, and I fortunately had a colleague I could refer him to.

ANTIDOTES TO PAINFUL MEMORIES

Like the model mugging classes that I discussed in chapter 13, the structures in psychomotor therapy hold out the possibility of forming virtual memories that live side by side with the painful realities of the past and provide sensory experiences of feeling seen, cradled, and supported that can serve as antidotes to memories of hurt and betrayal. In order to change, people need to become viscerally familiar with realities that directly contradict the static feelings of the frozen or panicked self of trauma, replacing them with sensations rooted in safety, mastery, delight, and connection. As we saw in the chapter on EMDR, one of the functions of dreaming is to create associations in which the frustrating events of the day are interwoven with the rest of one's life. Unlike our dreams, psychomotor structures are still subject to the laws of physics, but they too can reweave the past.

Of course we can never undo what happened, but we can create new emotional scenarios intense and real enough to defuse and counter some of those old ones. The healing tableaus of structures offer an experience that many participants have never believed was possible for them: to be welcomed into a world where people delight in them, protect them, meet their needs, and make you feel at home.

CHAPTER 19

REWIRING THE BRAIN:
NEUROFEEDBACK

Is it a fact—or have I dreamt it—that by means of electricity, the world of matter has become a great nerve, vibrating thousands of miles in a breathless point of time?

—**Nathaniel Hawthorne**

The faculty of voluntarily bringing back a wandering attention, over and over again, is the very root of the judgment, character, and will.

—**William James**

The summer after my first year of medical school, I worked as a part-time research assistant in Ernest Hartmann's sleep laboratory at Boston State Hospital. My job was to prepare and monitor the study participants and to analyze their EEG—electroencephalogram, or brain wave—tracings. Subjects would show up in the evening; I would paste an array of wires onto their scalps and another set of electrodes around their eyes to register the rapid eye movements that occur during dreaming. Then I would walk them to their bedrooms, bid them good night, and start the polygraph, a bulky machine with thirty-two pens that transmitted their brain activity onto a continuous spool of paper.

Even though our subjects were fast asleep, the neurons in their brains kept up their frenzied internal communication, which was transmitted to the polygraph throughout the night. I'd settle down to pore over the previous night's EEGs, stopping from time to time to pick up baseball scores on my radio, and use the intercom to wake subjects whenever the polygraph showed a REM sleep cycle. I would ask what they had dreamed about and write down what they reported and then in the morning help them fill out a questionnaire about sleep quality and send them on their way.

Those quiet nights at Hartmann's lab documented a great deal about REM sleep and contributed to building the basic understanding of sleep processes, which paved the way for the crucial discoveries that I discussed in chapter 15. However, until recently, the long-standing hope that the EEG would help us better understand how electrical brain activity contributes to psychiatric problems remained largely unrealized.

MAPPING THE ELECTRICAL CIRCUITS OF THE BRAIN

Before the advent of the pharmacological revolution, it was widely understood that brain activity depends on both chemical and electrical signals. The subsequent dominance of pharmacology almost obliterated interest in the electrophysiology of the brain for several decades.

The first recording of the brain's electrical activity was made in 1924 by the German psychiatrist Hans Berger. This new technology was initially met with skepticism and ridicule by the medical establishment, but electroencephalography gradually became an indispensable tool for diagnosing seizure activity in patients with epilepsy. Berger discovered that different brainwave patterns reflected different mental activities. (For example, trying to solve a math problem resulted in bursts at a moderately fast frequency band known as beta.) He hoped that eventually science would be able to correlate different psychiatric problems with specific EEG irregularities. This expectation was fueled by the first reports on EEG patterns in "behavior problem children" in 1938.[1] Most of these hyperactive and impulsive children had slower-than-normal waves in their frontal lobes. This finding has been reproduced innumerable times since then, and in 2013 slow-wave prefrontal activity was certified by the Food and Drug Administration as a biomarker for ADHD. Slow frontal lobe electrical activity explains why these kids have poor executive functioning: Their rational brains lack proper control over their emotional brains, which also occurs when abuse and trauma have made the emotional centers hyperalert to danger and organized for fight or flight.

Early in my career I also hoped that the EEG might help us to make better diagnoses, and between 1980 and 1990 I sent many of my patients to get EEGs to determine if their emotional instability was rooted in neurological abnormalities. The reports usually came back with the phrase: "nonspecific temporal lobe abnormalities."[2] This told me very little, and because at that time the only way we could change these ambiguous patterns was with drugs that had more side effects than benefits, I gave up doing routine EEGs on my patients.

Then, in 2000, a study by my friend Alexander McFarlane and his associates (researchers in Adelaide, Australia) rekindled my interest, as it documented clear differences in information processing between traumatized subjects and a group of "normal" Australians. The researchers used a standardized test called "the oddball paradigm" in which subjects are asked to detect the item that doesn't fit in a series of otherwise related images (like a trumpet in a group of tables and chairs). None of the images was related to trauma.

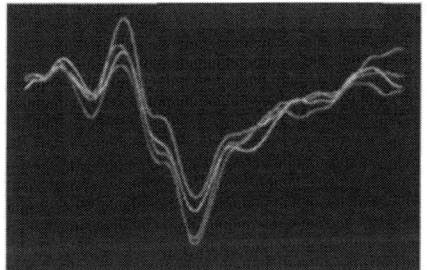 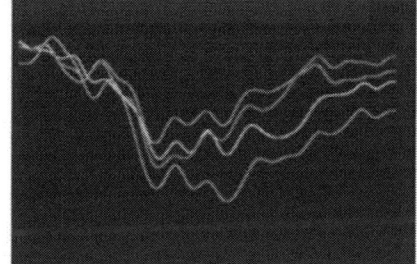

Normal versus PTSD. Patterns of attention. Milliseconds after the brain is presented with input it starts organizing the meaning of the incoming information. Normally, all regions of the brain collaborate in a synchronized pattern (left), while the brainwaves in PTSD are less well coordinated; the brain has trouble filtering out irrelevant information, and has problems attending to the stimulus at hand.

In the "normal" group key parts of the brain worked together to produce a coherent pattern of filtering, focus, and analysis. (See left image below.) In contrast, the brain waves of traumatized subjects were more loosely coordinated and failed to come together into a coherent pattern. Specifically, they did not generate the brainwave pattern that helps people pay attention on the task at hand by filtering out irrelevant information (the upward curve, labeled N200). In addition, the core information-processing configuration of the brain (the downward peak, P300) was poorly defined; the depth of the wave determines how well we are able to take in and analyze new data. This was important new information about how traumatized people process nontraumatic information that has profound implications for understanding day-to-day information processing. These brainwave patterns could explain why so many traumatized people have trouble learning from experience and fully engaging in their daily lives. Their brains are not organized to pay careful attention to what is going on in the present moment.

Sandy McFarlane's study reminded me of what Pierre Janet had said back in 1889: "Traumatic stress is an illness of not being able to be fully alive in the present." Years later, when I saw the movie *The Hurt Locker*, which dealt with the experiences of soldiers in Iraq, I immediately recalled Sandy's study: As long as they were coping with extreme stress, these men performed with pinpoint focus; but back in civilian life they were overwhelmed having to make simple choices in a supermarket. We are now seeing alarming statistics about the number of returning combat veterans who enroll in college on the GI Bill but do not complete their degrees. (Some estimates are over 80 percent.) Their well-documented problems with focusing and attention are surely contributing to these poor results.

McFarlane's study clarified a possible mechanism for the lack of focus and attention in PTSD, but it also presented a whole new challenge: Was there any way to change these dysfunctional brainwave patterns? It was seven years before I learned that there might be ways to do that.

In 2007 I met Sebern Fisher at a conference on attachment-disordered children. Sebern was the former clinical director of a residential treatment center for severely disturbed adolescents, and she told me that she'd been using neurofeedback in her private practice for about ten years. She showed me before-and-after drawings made by a ten-year-old. This boy had had such severe temper tantrums, learning disabilities, and overall difficulties with self-organization that he could not be handled in school.[3]

His first family portrait (on the left opposite), drawn before treatment started, was at the developmental level of a three-year-old. Less than five weeks later, after twenty sessions of neurofeedback, his tantrums had decreased and his drawing showed a marked improvement in complexity. Ten weeks and another twenty sessions later, his drawing took another leap in complexity and his behavior normalized.

I had never come across a treatment that could produce such a dramatic change in mental functioning in so brief a period of time. So when Sebern offered to give me a neurofeedback demonstration, I eagerly accepted.

SEEING THE SYMPHONY OF THE BRAIN

At Sebern's office in Northampton, Massachusetts, she showed me her neurofeedback equipment—two desktop computers and a small amplifier—and some of the data she had collected. She then pasted one electrode on each side of my skull and another on my right ear. Soon the computer in front of me was displaying rows of brain waves like the ones I'd seen on the sleep-lab polygraph three decades earlier. Sebern's tiny laptop could detect, record, and display the electrical symphony of my brain faster and more precisely than what had probably been a million dollars' worth of equipment in Hartmann's lab.

From stick figures to clearly defined human beings. After four months of neurofeedback, a ten-year-old boy's family drawings show the equivalent of six years of mental development.

As Sebern explained, feedback provides the brain with a mirror of its own function: the oscillations and rhythms that underpin the currents and crosscurrents of the mind. Neurofeedback nudges the brain to make more of some frequencies and less of others, creating new patterns that enhance its natural complexity and its bias toward self-regulation.[4] "In effect," she told me, "we may be freeing up innate but stuck oscillatory properties in the brain and allowing new ones to develop."

Sebern adjusted some settings, "to set the reward and inhibit frequencies," as she explained, so that the feedback would reinforce selected brainwave patterns while discouraging others. Now I was looking at something like a video game featuring three spaceships of different colors. The computer was emitting irregular tones, and the spaceships were moving quite randomly. I discovered that when I blinked my eyes they stopped, and when I calmly stared at the screen they moved in tandem, accompanied by regular beeps. Sebern then encouraged me to make the green spaceship move ahead of the others. I leaned forward to concentrate, but the harder I tried, the more the green spaceship fell behind. She smiled and told me that I'd do much better if I'd just relax and let my brain take in the feedback that the computer was generating. So I sat back, and after a while the tones grew steadier and the green spaceship started pulling ahead of the others. I felt calm and focused—and my spaceship was winning.

In some ways neurofeedback is similar to watching someone's face during a conversation. If you see smiles or slight nods, you're rewarded, and you go on telling your story or making your point. But the moment your conversation partner looks bored or shifts her gaze, you'll start to wrap up or change the topic. In neurofeedback the reward is a tone or movement on the screen instead of a smile, and the inhibition is far more neutral than a frown—it's simply an undesired pattern.

Next Sebern introduced another feature of neurofeedback: its ability to track circuitry in specific parts of the brain. She moved the electrodes from my temples to my left brow, and I started to feel sharp and focused. She told me she was rewarding beta waves in my frontal cortex, which accounted for my alertness. When she moved the electrodes to the crown of my head, I felt more detached from the computer images and more aware of the sensations in my body. Afterward she showed me a summary graph that recorded how my brain waves had changed as I experienced subtle shifts in my mental state and physical sensations.

How could neurofeedback be used to help to treat trauma? As Sebern explained: "With neurofeedback we hope to intervene in the circuitry that promotes and sustains states of fear and traits of fearfulness, shame, and rage. It is the repetitive firing of these circuits that defines trauma." Patients need help to change the habitual brain patterns created by trauma and its aftermath. When the fear patterns relax, the brain becomes less susceptible to automatic stress reactions and better able to focus on ordinary events. After all, stress is not an inherent property of events themselves—it is a function of how we label and react to them. Neurofeedback simply stabilizes the brain and increases resiliency, allowing us to develop more choices in how to respond.

THE BIRTH OF NEUROFEEDBACK

Neurofeedback was not a new technology in 2007. As early as the late 1950s University of Chicago psychology professor Joe Kamiya, who was studying the phenomenon of internal perception, had discovered that people could learn through feedback to tell when they were producing alpha waves, which are associated with relaxation. (It took some subjects only four days to reach 100 percent accuracy.) He then demonstrated that they could also enter voluntarily into an alpha state in response to a simple sound cue.

In 1968 an article about Kamiya's work was published in the popular magazine *Psychology Today*, and the idea that alpha training could relieve stress and stress-related conditions became widely known.[5] The first scientific work showing that neurofeedback could have an effect on pathological conditions was done by Barry Sterman at UCLA. The National Aeronautics and Space Administration had asked Sterman to study the toxicity of a rocket fuel, monomethylhydrazine (MMH), which was known to cause hallucinations, nausea, and seizures. Sterman had previously trained some cats to produce a specific EEG frequency known as the sensorimotor rhythm. (In cats this alert, focused state is associated with waiting to be fed.) He discovered that while his ordinary lab cats developed seizures after exposure to MMH, the cats that had received neurofeedback did not. The training had somehow stabilized their brains.

In 1971 Sterman attached his first human subject, twenty-three-year-old Mary Fairbanks, to a neurofeedback device. She had suffered from epilepsy since the age of eight, with grand mal seizures two or more times a month. She trained for an hour a day twice a week. At the end of three months she was virtually seizure free. Sterman subsequently received a grant from the National Institutes of Health to conduct a more systematic study, and the impressive results were published in the journal *Epilepsia* in 1978.[6]

This period of experimentation and huge optimism about the potential of the human mind came to an end in the middle 1970s with newly discovered psychiatric drugs. Psychiatry and brain science adopted a chemical model of mind and brain, and other treatment approaches were relegated to the back burner.

Since then the field of neurofeedback has grown by fits and starts, with much of the scientific groundwork being done in Europe, Russia, and Australia. Even though there are about ten thousand neurofeedback practitioners in the United States, the practice has not been able to garner the research funding necessary to gain widespread acceptance. One reason may be that there are multiple competing neurofeedback systems; another is that the commercial potential is limited. Only a few applications are covered by insurance, which makes neurofeedback expensive for consumers and prevents practitioners from amassing the resources necessary to do large-scale studies.

FROM A HOMELESS SHELTER TO THE NURSING STATION

Sebern had arranged for me to speak with three of her patients. All told remarkable stories, but as I listened to twenty-seven-year-old Lisa, who was studying nursing at a nearby college, I felt myself truly awakening to the stunning potential of this treatment. Lisa possessed the greatest single resilience factor humans can have: She was an appealing person—engaging, curious, and obviously intelligent. She made great eye contact, and she was eager to share what she had learned about herself. Best of all, like so many survivors I've known, she had a wry sense of humor and a delicious take on human folly.

Based on what I knew about her background, it was a miracle that she was so calm and self-possessed. She had spent years in group homes and mental hospitals, and she was a familiar presence in the emergency rooms of western Massachusetts—the girl who regularly arrived by ambulance, half dead from prescription drug overdoses or bloody from self-inflicted wounds.

Here is how she began her story: "I used to envy the kids who knew what would happen when their parents got drunk. At least they could predict the havoc. In my home there was no pattern. Anything could set my mother off—eating dinner, watching TV, coming home from school, getting dressed—and I never knew what she was going to do or how she would hurt me. It was so random."

Her father had abandoned the family when Lisa was three years old, leaving her at the mercy of her psychotic mother. "Torture" is not too strong a word to describe the abuse she endured. "I lived up in the attic room," she told me, "and there was another room up there where I would go and piss on the carpet because I was too scared to go downstairs to the bathroom. I would take all the clothes off my dolls and drive pencils into them and put them up in my window."

When she was twelve years old, Lisa ran away from home and was picked up by the police and returned. After she ran away again, child protective services stepped in, and she spent the next six years in mental hospitals, shelters, group homes, foster families, and on the street. No placement lasted, because Lisa was so dissociated and self-destructive that she terrified her caretakers. She would attack herself or destroy furniture and afterward she would not remember what she had done, which earned her a reputation as a manipulative liar. In retrospect, Lisa told me, she simply lacked the language to communicate what was going on with her.

When she turned eighteen, she "matured out" of child protective services and started an independent life, one without family, education, money, or skills. But shortly after discharge she ran into Sebern, who had just acquired her first neurofeedback equipment and remembered Lisa from the residential treatment center where she had once worked. She'd always had a soft spot for this lost girl, and she invited Lisa to try out her new gizmo.

As Sebern recalled: "When Lisa first came to see me, it was fall. She walked around with a vacant stare, carrying a pumpkin wherever she went. There just wasn't a there there. I wasn't ever sure that I had gotten to any organizing self." Any form of talk therapy was impossible for Lisa. Whenever Sebern asked her about anything stressful, she would shut down or go into a panic. In Lisa's words: "Every time we tried to talk about what had happened to me growing up, I would have a breakdown. I would wake up with cuts and burns and I wouldn't be able to eat. I wouldn't be able to sleep."

Her sense of terror was omnipresent: "I was afraid all the time. I didn't like to be touched. I was always jumpy and nervous. I couldn't close my eyes if another person was around. There was no convincing me that someone wasn't going to kick me the second I closed my eyes. That makes you feel crazy. You know you're in a room with someone you trust, you know intellectually that nothing's going to happen to you, but then there's the rest of your body and you can't ever relax. If someone put their arm around me, I would just check out." She was stuck in a state of inescapable shock.

Lisa recalled dissociating when she was a little girl, but things got worse after puberty: "I started waking up with cuts, and people at school would know me by different names. I couldn't have a steady boyfriend because I would date other guys when I was dissociated and then not remember. I was blacking out a lot and opening my eyes into some pretty strange situations." Like many severely traumatized people, Lisa could not recognize herself in a mirror.[7] I had never heard anyone describe so articulately what it was like to lack a continuous sense of self.

There was no one to confirm her reality. "When I was seventeen and living in the group home for severely disturbed adolescents, I cut myself up really badly with the lid of a tin can. They took me to the emergency room, but I couldn't tell the doctor what I had done to cut myself—I didn't have any memory of it. The ER doctor was convinced that dissociative identity disorder didn't exist. . . . A lot of people involved in mental health tell you it doesn't exist. Not that you don't have it, but that it doesn't exist."

The first thing Lisa did after she aged out of her residential treatment program was to go off her medications: "This doesn't work for everybody," she acknowledged, "but it turned out to be personally the right choice. I know people who need meds, but that was not the case for me. After going off them and starting neurofeedback, I became much clearer."

When she invited Lisa to do neurofeedback, Sebern had little idea what to expect, as Lisa would be the first dissociative patient she tried it on. They met twice a week and started by rewarding more coherent brain patterns in the right temporal lobe, the fear center of the brain. After a few weeks Lisa noticed she was wasn't as uptight around people, and she no longer dreaded the basement laundry room in her building. Then came a bigger breakthrough: She stopped dissociating. "I'd always had a constant hum of low-level conversations in my head," she recalled. "I was scared I was schizophrenic. After half a year of neurofeedback I stopped hearing those noises. I integrated, I guess. Everything just came together."

As Lisa developed a more continuous sense of self, she became able to talk about her experiences: "I now can actually talk about things like my childhood. For the first time I started being able to *do* therapy. Up till then I didn't have enough distance and I couldn't calm down enough. If you're still in it, it's hard to talk about it. I wasn't able to attach in the way that you need to attach and open up in the way that you need to open up in order to have any type of relationship with a therapist." This was a stunning revelation: So many patients are in and out of treatment, unable to meaningfully connect because they are still "in it." Of course, when people don't know who they are, they can't possibly see the reality of the people around them.

Lisa went on: "There was so much anxiety around attachment. I would go into a room and try to memorize every possible way to get out, every detail about a person. I was trying desperately to keep track of everything that could hurt me. Now I know people in a different way. It's not based on memorizing them out of fear. When you're not afraid of being hurt, you can know people differently."

This articulate young woman had emerged from the depths of despair and confusion with a degree of clarity and focus I had never seen before. It was clear that we had to explore the potential of neurofeedback at the Trauma Center.

GETTING STARTED IN NEUROFEEDBACK

First we had to decide which of five different existing neurofeedback systems to adopt, and then find a long weekend to learn the principles and practice on one another.[8] Eight staff members and three trainers volunteered their time to explore the complexities of EEGs, electrodes, and computer-generated feedback. On the second morning of the training, when I was partnered with my colleague Michael, I placed an electrode on the right side of his head, directly over the sensorimotor strip of his brain, and rewarded the frequency of eleven to fourteen hertz. Shortly after the session ended, Michael asked for the attention of the group. He'd just had a remarkable experience, he told us. He had always felt somewhat on edge and unsafe in the presence of other people, even colleagues like us. Although nobody seemed to notice—he was, after all, a well-respected therapist—he lived with a chronic, gnawing sense of danger. That feeling was now gone, and he felt safe, relaxed, and open. Over the next three years Michael emerged from his habitual low profile to challenge the group with his insights and opinions, and he became one of the most valuable contributors to our neurofeedback program.

With the help of the ANS Foundation we started our first study with a group of seventeen patients who had not responded to previous treatments. We targeted the right temporal area of the brain, the location that our early brain-scan studies (described in chapter 3)[9] had shown to be excessively activated during traumatic stress, and gave them twenty neurofeedback sessions over ten weeks.

Because most of these patients suffered from alexithymia, it was not easy for them to report their response to the treatments. But their actions spoke for them: They consistently showed up on time for their appointments, even if they had to drive through snowstorms. None of them dropped out, and at the end of the full twenty sessions, we could document significant improvements not only in their PTSD scores,[10] but also in their interpersonal comfort, emotional balance, and self-awareness.[11] They were less frantic, they slept better, and they felt calmer and more focused.

In any case, self-reports can be unreliable; objective changes in behavior are much better indicators of how well treatment works. The first patient I treated with neurofeedback was a good example. He was a professional man in his early fifties who defined himself as heterosexual, but he compulsively sought homosexual contact with strangers whenever he felt abandoned and misunderstood. His marriage had broken up around this issue, and he had become HIV positive; he was desperate to gain control over his behavior. During a previous therapy he had talked extensively about his sexual abuse by an uncle at around the age of eight. We assumed that his compulsion was related to that abuse, but making that connection had made no difference in his behavior. After more than a year of regular psychotherapy with a competent therapist, nothing had changed.

A week after I started to train his brain to produce slower waves in his right temporal lobe, he had a distressing argument with a new girlfriend, and instead of going to his habitual cruising spot to find sex he decided to go fishing. I attributed that response to chance. However, over the next ten weeks, in the midst of his tumultuous relationship, he continued to find solace in fishing and began to renovate a lakeside cabin. When we skipped three weeks of neurofeedback because of our vacations schedules, his compulsion suddenly returned, suggesting that his brain had not yet stabilized its new pattern. We trained for six more months, and now, four years later, I see him about every six months for a checkup. He has felt no further impulse to engage in his dangerous sexual activities.

How did his brain come to derive comfort from fishing rather than from compulsive sexual behavior? At this point we simply don't know. Neurofeedback changes brain connectivity patterns; the mind follows by creating new patterns of engagement.

BRAINWAVE BASICS FROM SLOW TO FAST

Each line on an EEG charts the activity in a different part of the brain: a mixture of different rhythms, ranged on a scale from slow to fast.[12] The EEG consists of measurements of varying heights (amplitude) and wavelengths (frequency).

Frequency refers to the number of times a waveform rises and falls in one second, and it is measured in hertz (Hz), or cycles per second (cps). Every frequency on the EEG is relevant to understanding and treating trauma, and the basics are relatively easy to grasp.

Delta waves, the slowest frequencies (2–5 Hz) are seen most often during sleep. The brain is in an idling state, and the mind is turned inward. If people have too much slow-wave activity while they're awake, their thinking is foggy and they exhibit poor judgment and poor impulse control. Eighty percent of children with ADHD and many individuals diagnosed with PTSD have excessive slow waves in their frontal lobes.

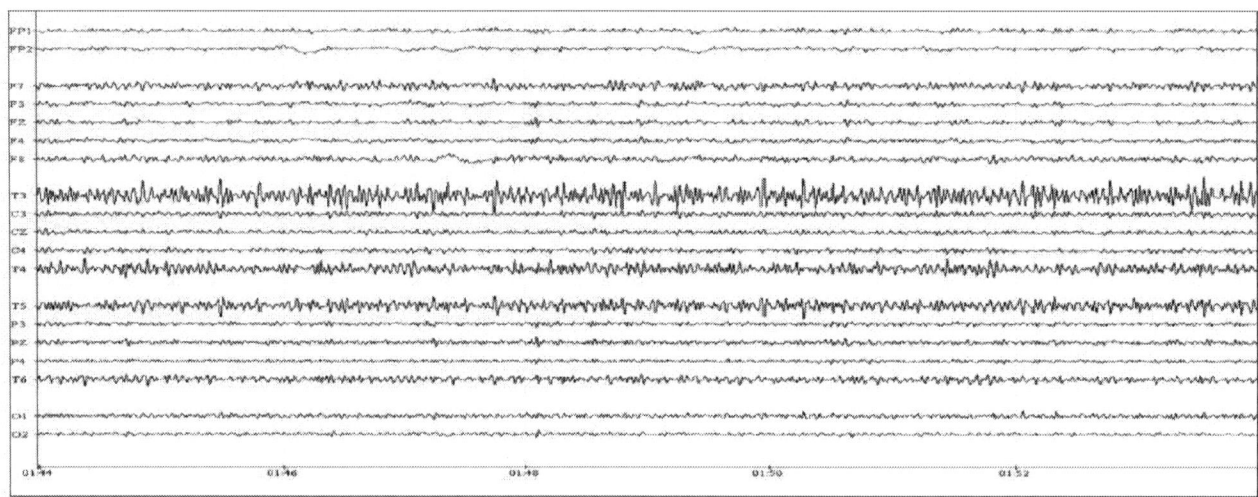

The Electroencephalogram (EEG). While there is no typical signature for PTSD, many traumatized people have sharply increased activity in the temporal lobes, as this patient does (T_3, T_4, T_5). Neurofeedback can normalize these abnormal brain patterns and thereby increase emotional stability.

THE RATE OF BRAINWAVE FIRING IS RELATED TO OUR STATE OF AROUSAL

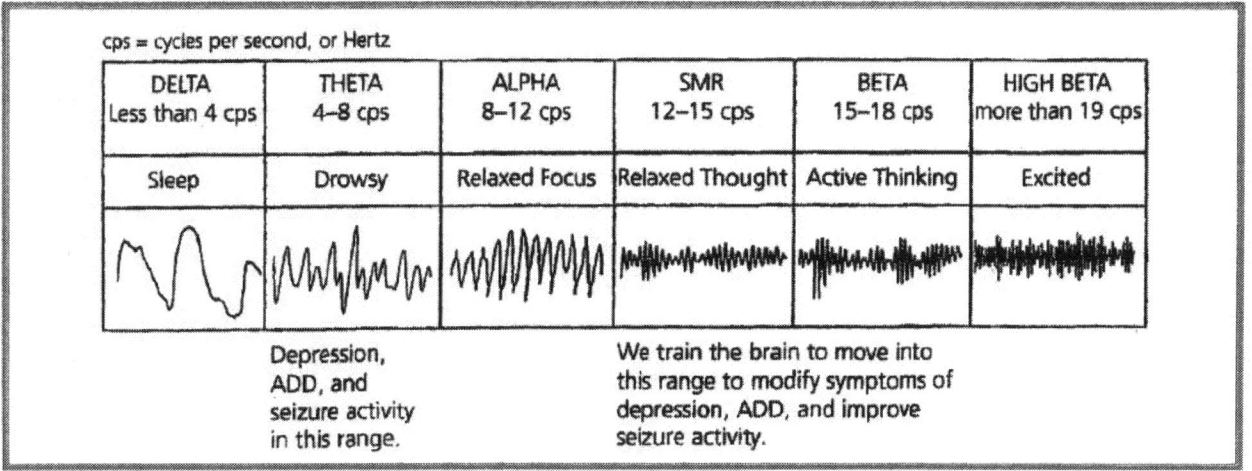

DELTA Less than 4 cps	THETA 4–8 cps	ALPHA 8–12 cps	SMR 12–15 cps	BETA 15–18 cps	HIGH BETA more than 19 cps
Sleep	Drowsy	Relaxed Focus	Relaxed Thought	Active Thinking	Excited

cps = cycles per second, or Hertz

Depression, ADD, and seizure activity in this range.

We train the brain to move into this range to modify symptoms of depression, ADD, and improve seizure activity.

Dreaming speeds up brain waves. Theta frequencies (5–8 Hz) predominate at the edge of sleep, as in the floating "hypnopompic" state I described in chapter 15 on EMDR; they are also characteristic of hypnotic trance states. Theta waves create a frame of mind unconstrained by logic or by the ordinary demands of life and thus open the potential for making novel connections and associations. One of the most promising EEG neurofeedback treatments for PTSD, alpha/theta training, makes use of that quality to loosen frozen associations and facilitate new learning. On the downside, theta frequencies also occur when we're "out of it" or depressed.

Alpha waves (8–12 Hz) are accompanied by a sense of peace and calm.[13] They are familiar to anyone who has learned mindfulness meditation. (A patient once told me that neurofeedback worked for him "like meditation on steroids.") I use alpha training most often in my practice to help people who are either too numb or too agitated to achieve a state of focused relaxation. Walter Reed National Military Medical Center recently introduced alpha-training instruments to treat soldiers with PTSD, but at the time of this writing the results are not yet available.

Beta waves are the fastest frequencies (13–20 Hz). When they dominate, the brain is oriented to the outside world. Beta enables us to engage in focused attention while performing a task. However, high beta (over 20 Hz) is associated with agitation, anxiety, and body tenseness—in effect, we are constantly scanning the environment for danger.

HELPING THE BRAIN TO FOCUS

Neurofeedback training can improve creativity, athletic control, and inner awareness, even in people who already are highly accomplished.[14] When we started to study neurofeedback, we discovered that sports medicine was the only department in Boston University that had any familiarity with the subject. One of my earliest teachers in brain physiology was the sports psychologist Len Zaichkowsky, who soon left Boston to train the Vancouver Canucks with neurofeedback.[15]

Neurofeedback has probably been studied more thoroughly for performance enhancement than for psychiatric problems. In Italy the trainer for the soccer club AC Milan used it to help players remain relaxed and focused as they watched videos of their errors. Their increased mental and physiological control paid off when several players joined the Italian team that won the 2006 World Cup—and when AC Milan won the European championship the following year.[16] Neurofeedback was also included in the science and technology component of Own the Podium, a $117 million, five-year plan engineered to help Canada dominate the 2010 Winter Olympics in Vancouver. The Canadians won the most gold medals and came in third overall.

Musical performance has been shown to benefit as well. A panel of judges from Britain's Royal College of Music found that students who were trained with ten sessions of neurofeedback by John Gruzelier of the University of London had a 10 percent improvement in the performance of a piece of music, compared with students who had not received neurofeedback. This represents a huge difference in such a competitive field.[17]

Given its enhancement of focus, attention, and concentration, it's not surprising that neurofeedback drew the attention of specialists in attention-deficit/hyperactivity disorder (ADHD). At least thirty-six studies have shown that neurofeedback can be an effective and time-limited treatment for ADHD—one that's about as effective as conventional drugs.[18] Once the brain has been trained to produce different patterns of electrical communication, no further treatment is necessary, in contrast to drugs, which do not change fundamental brain activity and work only as long as the patient keeps taking them.

WHERE IS THE PROBLEM IN MY BRAIN?

Sophisticated computerized EEG analysis, known as the quantitative EEG (qEEG), can trace brainwave activity millisecond by millisecond, and its software can convert that activity into a color map that shows which frequencies are highest or lowest in key areas of the brain.[19] The qEEG can also show how well brain regions are communicating or working together. Several large qEEG databases of both normal and abnormal patterns are available, which allows us to compare a patient's qEEG with those of thousands of other people with similar issues. Last but not least, in contrast to fMRIs and related scans, the qEEG is both relatively inexpensive and portable.

The qEEG provides compelling evidence of the arbitrary boundaries of current DSM diagnostic categories. DSM labels for mental illness are not aligned with specific patterns of brain activation. Mental states that are common to many diagnoses, such as confusion, agitation, or feeling disembodied, are associated with specific patterns on the qEEG. In general, the more problems a patient has, the more abnormalities show up in the qEEG.[20]

Our patients find it very helpful to be able to see the patterns of localized electrical activity in their brains. We can show them the patterns that seem to be responsible for their difficulty focusing or for their lack of emotional control. They can see why different brain areas need to be trained to generate different frequencies and communication patterns. These explanations help them shift from self-blaming attempts to control their behavior to learning to process information differently.

As Ed Hamlin, who trained us in interpreting the qEEG, recently wrote to me: "Many people respond to the training, but the ones that respond best and quickest are those that can see how the feedback is related to something they are doing. For example, if I'm attempting to help someone increase their ability to be present, we can see how they're doing with it. Then the benefit really begins to accumulate. There is something very empowering about having the experience of changing your brain's activity with your mind."

HOW DOES TRAUMA CHANGE BRAIN WAVES?

In our neurofeedback lab we see individuals with long histories of traumatic stress who have only partially responded to existing treatments. Their qEEGs show a variety of different patterns. Often there is excessive activity in the right temporal lobe, the fear center of the brain, combined with too much frontal slow-wave activity. This means that their hyperaroused emotional brains dominate their mental life. Our research showed that calming the fear center decreases trauma-based problems and improves executive functioning. This is reflected not only in a significant decrease in patients' PTSD scores but also in improved mental clarity and an increased ability to regulate how upset they become in response to relatively minor provocations.[21]

Other traumatized patients show patterns of hyperactivity the moment they close their eyes: Not seeing what is going on around them makes them panic and their brain waves go wild. We train them to produce more relaxed brain patterns. Yet another group overreacts to sounds and light, a sign that the thalamus has difficulty filtering out irrelevant information. In those patients we focus on changing communication patterns at the back of the brain.

While our center is focused on finding optimal treatments for long-standing traumatic stress, Alexander McFarlane is studying how exposure to combat changes previously normal brains. The Australian Department of Defence asked his research group to measure the effects of deployment to combat duty in Iraq and Afghanistan on mental and biological functioning, including brainwave patterns. In the initial phase McFarlane and his colleagues measured the qEEG in 179 combat troops four months prior to and four months after each successive deployment to the Middle East.

They found that the total number of months in combat over a three-year period was associated with progressive decreases in alpha power at the back of the brain. This area, which monitors the state of the body and regulates such elementary processes as sleep and hunger, ordinarily has the highest level of alpha waves of any region in the brain, particularly when people close their eyes. As we have seen, alpha is associated with relaxation. The decrease in alpha power in these soldiers reflects a state of persistent agitation. At the same time the brain waves at the front of the brain, which normally have high levels of beta, show a progressive slowing with each deployment. The soldiers gradually develop frontal-lobe activity that resembles that of children with ADHD, which interferes with their executive functioning and capacity for focused attention.

The net effect is that arousal, which is supposed to provide us with the energy needed to engage in day-to-day tasks, no longer helps these soldiers to focus on ordinary tasks. It simply makes them agitated and restless. At this stage of McFarlane's study, it is too early to know if any of these soldiers will develop PTSD, and only time will tell to what degree these brains will readjust to the pace of civilian life.

NEUROFEEDBACK AND LEARNING DISABILITIES

Chronic abuse and neglect in childhood interfere with the proper wiring of sensory-integration systems. In some cases this results in learning disabilities, which include faulty connections between the auditory and word-processing systems, and poor hand-eye coordination. As long as they are frozen or explosive, it is difficult to see how much trouble the adolescents in our residential treatment programs have processing day-to-day information, but once their behavioral problems have been successfully treated, their learning disabilities often become manifest. Even if these traumatized kids could sit still and pay attention, many of them would still be handicapped by their poor learning skills.[22]

Lisa described how trauma had interfered with the proper wiring of basic processing functions. She told me she "always got lost" going places, and she recalled having a marked auditory delay that kept her from being able to follow the instructions from her teachers. "Imagine being in a classroom," she said, "and the teacher comes in and says, 'Good morning. Turn to page two-seventy-two. Do problems one to five.' If you're even a fraction of a second off, it's just a jumble. It was impossible to concentrate."

Neurofeedback helped her to reverse these learning disabilities. "I learned to keep track of things; for example, to read maps. Right after we started therapy, there was this memorable time when I was going from Amherst to Northampton [less than ten miles] to meet Sebern. I was supposed to take a couple of buses, but I ended up walking along the highway for a couple miles. I was that disorganized—I couldn't read the schedule; I couldn't keep track of the time. I was too jacked up and nervous, which made me tired all the time. I couldn't pay attention and keep it together. I just couldn't organize my brain around it."

That statement defines the challenge for brain and mind science: How can we help people learn to organize time and space, distance and relationships, capacities that are laid down in the brain during the first few years of life, if early trauma has interfered with their development? Neither drugs nor conventional therapy have been shown to activate the neuroplasticity necessary to bring those capacities online after the critical periods have passed. Now is the time to study whether neurofeedback can succeed where other interventions have failed.

ALPHA-THETA TRAINING

Alpha-theta training is a particularly fascinating neurofeedback procedure, because it can induce the sorts of hypnagogic states—the essence of hypnotic trance—that are discussed in chapter 15.[23] When theta waves predominate in the brain, the mind's focus is on the internal world, a world of free-floating imagery. Alpha brain waves may act as a bridge from the external world to the internal, and vice versa. In alpha-theta training these frequencies are alternately rewarded.

The challenge in PTSD is to open the mind to new possibilities, so that the present is no longer interpreted as a continuous reliving of the past. Trance states, during which theta activity dominates, can help to loosen the conditioned connections between particular stimuli and responses, such as loud cracks signaling gunfire, a harbinger of death. A new association can be created in which that same crack can come to be linked to Fourth of July fireworks at the end of a day at the beach with loved ones.

In the twilight states fostered by alpha/theta training, traumatic events may be safely reexperienced and new associations fostered. Some patients report unusual imagery and/or deep insights about their life; others simply become more relaxed and less rigid. Any state in which people can safely experience images, feelings, and emotions that are associated with dread and helplessness is likely to create fresh potential and a wider perspective.

Can alpha-theta reverse hyperarousal patterns? The accumulated evidence is promising. Eugene Peniston and Paul Kulkosky, researchers at the VA Medical Center in Fort Lyon, Colorado, used neurofeedback to treat twenty-nine Vietnam veterans with a twelve-to- fifteen-year history of chronic combat-related PTSD. Fifteen of the men were randomly assigned to the EEG alpha-theta training and fourteen to a control group that received standard medical care, including psychotropic drugs and individual and group therapy. On average, participants in both groups had been hospitalized more than five times for their PTSD. The neurofeedback facilitated twilight states of learning by rewarding both alpha and theta waves. As the men lay back in a recliner with their eyes closed, they were coached to allow the neurofeedback sounds to guide them into deep relaxation. They were also asked to use positive mental imagery (for example, being sober, living confidently and happily) as they moved toward the trancelike alpha-theta state.

This study, published in 1991, had one of the best outcomes ever recorded for PTSD. The neurofeedback group had a significant decrease in their PTSD symptoms, as well as in physical complaints, depression, anxiety, and paranoia. After the treatment phase the veterans and their family members were contacted monthly for a period of thirty months. Only three of the fifteen neurofeedback-treated veterans reported disturbing flashbacks and nightmares. All three chose to undergo ten booster sessions; only one needed to return to the hospital for further treatment. Fourteen out of fifteen were using significantly less medication.

In contrast, every vet in the comparison group experienced an increase in PTSD symptoms during the follow-up period, and all of them required at least two further hospitalizations. Ten of the comparison group also increased their medication use.[24] This study has been replicated by other researchers, but it has received surprisingly little attention outside the neurofeedback community.[25]

NEUROFEEDBACK, PTSD, AND ADDICTION

Approximately one-third to one-half of severely traumatized people develop substance abuse problems.[26] Since the time of Homer, soldiers have used alcohol to numb their pain, irritability, and depression. In one recent study half of motor vehicle accident victims developed problems with drugs or alcohol. Alcohol abuse makes people careless and thus increases their chances of being traumatized again (although being drunk during an assault actually decreases the likelihood of developing PTSD).

There is a circular relationship between PTSD and substance abuse: While drugs and alcohol may provide temporary relief from trauma symptoms, withdrawing from them increases hyperarousal, thereby intensifying nightmares, flashbacks, and irritability. There are only two ways to end this vicious cycle: by resolving the symptoms of PTSD with methods such as EMDR or by treating the hyperarousal that is part of both PTSD and withdrawal from drugs or alcohol. Drugs such as naltrexone are sometimes prescribed to reduce hyperarousal, but this treatment helps in only some cases.

One of the first women I trained with neurofeedback had a long-standing cocaine addiction, in addition to a horrendous childhood history of sexual abuse and abandonment. Much to my surprise, her cocaine habit cleared after the first two sessions and on follow-up five years later had not returned. I had never seen anyone recover this quickly from severe drug abuse, so I turned to the existing scientific literature for guidance.[27] Most of the studies on this subject were done more than two decades ago; in recent years, very few neurofeedback studies for the treatment of addiction have been published, at least in the United States.

Between 75 percent and 80 percent of patients who are admitted for detox and alcohol and drug abuse treatment will relapse. Another study by Peniston and Kulkosky—on the effects of neurofeedback training with veterans who had dual diagnoses of alcoholism and PTSD[28]—focused on this problem. Fifteen veterans received alpha-theta training, while the control group received standard treatment without neurofeedback. The subjects were followed up regularly for three years, during which eight members of neurofeedback group stopped drinking completely and one got drunk once but became sick and didn't drink again. Most of them were markedly less depressed. As Peniston put it, the changes reported corresponded to being "more warmhearted, more intelligent, more emotionally stable, more socially bold, more relaxed and more satisfied."[29] In contrast, all of those given standard treatment were readmitted to the hospital within eighteen months.[30] Since that time a number of studies on neurofeedback for addictions have been published,[31] but this important application needs much more research to establish its potential and limitations.

THE FUTURE OF NEUROFEEDBACK

In my practice I use neurofeedback primarily to help with the hyperarousal, confusion, and concentration problems of people who suffer from developmental trauma. However, it has also shown good results for numerous issues and conditions that go beyond the scope of this book, including relieving tension headaches, improving cognitive functioning following a traumatic brain injury, reducing anxiety and panic attacks, learning to deepen meditation states, treating autism, improving seizure control, self-regulation in mood disorders, and more. As of 2013 neurofeedback is being used in seventeen military and VA facilities to treat PTSD,[32] and scientific documentation of its efficacy in recent combat vets is just beginning to be assessed. Frank Duffy, the director of the clinical neurophysiology and developmental neurophysiology laboratories of Boston Children's Hospital, has commented: "The literature, which lacks any negative study, suggests that neurofeedback plays a major therapeutic role in many different areas. In my opinion, if any medication had demonstrated such a wide spectrum of efficacy it would be universally accepted and widely used."[33]

Many questions remain to be answered about treatment protocols for neurofeedback, but the scientific paradigm is gradually shifting in a direction that invites a deeper exploration of these questions. In 2010 Thomas Insel, director of the National Institute of Mental Health, published an article in *Scientific American* entitled "Faulty Circuits," in which he called for a return to understanding mind and brain in terms of the rhythms and patterns of electrical communication: "Brain regions that function together to carry out normal (and abnormal) mental operations can be thought of as analogous to electrical circuits—the latest research shows that the malfunctioning of entire circuits may underlie many mental disorders."[34] Three years later Insel announced that NIMH was "re-orienting its research away from DSM categories"[35] and focusing instead on "disorders of the human connectome."[36]

As explained by Francis Collins, director of the National Institutes of Health (of which NIMH is a part), "The connectome refers to the exquisitely interconnected network of neurons (nerve cells) in your brain. Like the genome, the microbiome, and other exciting 'ome' fields, the effort to map the connectome and decipher the electrical signals that zap through it to generate your thoughts, feelings, and behaviors has become possible through development of powerful new tools and technologies."[37] The connectome is now being mapped in detail under the auspices of NIMH.

As we await the results of this research, I'd like to give the last word to Lisa, the survivor who introduced me to the enormous potential of neurofeedback. When I asked her to summarize what the treatment had done for her, she said: "It calmed me down. It stopped the dissociation. I can use my feelings; I'm not running away from them. I'm not held hostage by them. I can't turn them off and on, but I can put them away. I may be sad about the abuse I went through, but I can put it away. I can call a friend and not talk about it if I don't want to talk about it, or I can do homework or clean my apartment. Emotions mean something now. I'm not anxious all the time, and when I am anxious, I can reflect on it. If the anxiety's coming from the past, I can find it there, or I can look at how it relates to my life now. And it's not just negative emotions, like anger and anxiety—I can reflect on love and intimacy or sexual attraction. I'm not in fight-or-flight all the time. My blood pressure is down. I'm not physically prepared to take off at any moment or defend myself against an attack. Neurofeedback made it possible for me to have a relationship. Neurofeedback freed me up to live my life the way I want to, because I'm not always in the thrall of how I was hurt and what it did to me."

Four years after I met her and recorded our conversations, Lisa graduated near the top of her nursing school class, and she now works full time as a nurse at a local hospital.

CHAPTER 20

FINDING YOUR VOICE: COMMUNAL RHYTHMS AND THEATER

Acting is not about putting on a character but discovering the character within you: you are the character, you just have to find it within yourself—albeit a very expanded version of yourself.

—**Tina Packer**

Many scientists I know were inspired by their children's health problems to find new ways of understanding mind, brain, and therapy. My own son's recovery from a mysterious illness that, for lack of a better name, we call chronic fatigue syndrome, convinced me of the therapeutic possibilities of theater.

Nick spent most of seventh and eighth grade in bed, bloated by allergies and medications that left him too exhausted to go to school. His mother and I saw him becoming entrenched in his identity as a self-hating and isolated kid, and we were desperate to help him. When his mother realized that he picked up a little energy round 5:00 p.m., we signed him up for an evening class in improvisational theater where he would at least have a chance to interact with other boys and girls his age. He took to the group and to the acting exercises and soon landed his first role, as Action in *West Side Story*, a tough kid who's always ready to fight and has the lead in singing "Gee, Officer Krupke." One day at home I caught him walking with a swagger, practicing what it was like to be somebody with clout. Was he developing a physical sense of pleasure, imagining himself as a strong guy who commands respect?

Then he was cast as the Fonz in *Happy Days*. Being adored by girls and keeping an audience spellbound became the real tipping point in his recovery. Unlike his experience with the numerous therapists who had talked with him about how bad he felt, theater gave him a chance to deeply and physically experience what it was like to be someone other than the learning-disabled, oversensitive boy that he had gradually become. Being a valued contributor to a group gave him a visceral experience of power and competence. I believe that this new embodied version of himself set him on the road to becoming the creative, loving adult he is today.

Our sense of agency, how much we feel in control, is defined by our relationship with our bodies and its rhythms: Our waking and sleeping and how we eat, sit, and walk define the contours of our days. In order to find our voice, we have to be *in* our bodies—able to breathe fully and able to access our inner sensations. This is the opposite of dissociation, of being "out of body" and making yourself disappear. It's also the opposite of depression, lying slumped in front of a screen that provides passive entertainment. Acting is an experience of using your body to take your place in life.

THE THEATER OF WAR

Nick's transformation was not the first time I'd witnessed the benefits of theater. In 1988 I was still treating three veterans with PTSD whom I'd met at the VA, and when they showed a sudden improvement in their vitality, optimism, and family relationships, I attributed it to my growing therapeutic skills. Then I discovered that all three were involved in a theatrical production.

Wanting to dramatize the plight of homeless veterans, they had persuaded playwright David Mamet, who was living nearby, to meet weekly with their group to develop a script around their experiences. Mamet then recruited Al Pacino, Donald Sutherland, and Michael J. Fox to come to Boston for an evening called *Sketches of War*, which raised money to convert the VA clinic where I'd met my patients into a shelter for homeless veterans.[1] Standing on a stage with professional actors, speaking about their memories of the war, and reading their poetry was clearly a more transformative experience than any therapy could have offered them.

Since time immemorial human beings have used communal rituals to cope with their most powerful and terrifying feelings. Ancient Greek theater, the oldest of which we have written records, seems to have grown out of religious rites that involved dancing, singing, and reenacting mythical stories. By the fifth century BCE, theater played a central role in civic life, with the audience seated in a horseshoe around the stage, which enabled them to see one another's emotions and reactions.

Greek drama may have served as a ritual reintegration for combat veterans. At the time Aeschylus wrote the *Oresteia* trilogy, Athens was at war on six fronts; the cycle of tragedy is set in motion when the returning warrior king Agamemnon is murdered by his wife, Clytemnestra, for having sacrificed their daughter before sailing to the Trojan War. Military service was required of every adult citizen of Athens, so audiences were undoubtedly composed of combat veterans and active-duty soldiers on leave. The performers themselves must have been citizen-soldiers.

Sophocles was a general officer in Athens's wars against the Persians, and his play *Ajax*, which ends with the suicide of one of the Trojan War's greatest heroes, reads like a textbook description of traumatic stress. In 2008 writer and director Bryan Doerries arranged a reading of *Ajax* for five hundred marines in San Diego and was stunned by the reception it received. (Like many of us who work with trauma, Doerries's inspiration was personal; he had studied classics in college and turned to the Greek texts for comfort when he lost a girlfriend to cystic fibrosis.) His project "The Theater of War" evolved from that first event, and with funding from the U.S. Department of Defense, this 2,500-year-old play has since been performed more than two hundred times here and abroad to give voice to the plight of combat veterans and foster dialogue and understanding in their families and friends.[2]

Theater of War performances are followed by a town hall–style discussion. I attended a reading of *Ajax* in Cambridge, Massachusetts, shortly after the news media had publicized a 27 percent increase in suicides among combat veterans over the previous three years. Some forty people—Vietnam veterans, military wives, recently discharged men and women who had served in Iraq and Afghanistan—lined up behind the microphone. Many of them quoted lines from the play as they spoke about their sleepless nights, drug addiction, and alienation from their families. The atmosphere was electric, and afterward the audience huddled in the foyer, some holding each other and crying, others in deep conversation.

As Doerries later said: "Anyone who has come into contact with extreme pain, suffering or death has no trouble understanding Greek drama. It's all about bearing witness to the stories of veterans."[3]

KEEPING TOGETHER IN TIME

Collective movement and music create a larger context for our lives, a meaning beyond our individual fate. Religious rituals universally involve rhythmic movements, from davening at the Wailing Wall in Jerusalem to the sung liturgy and gestures of the Catholic Mass to moving meditation in Buddhist ceremonies and the rhythmic prayer rituals performed five times a day by devout Muslims.

Music was a backbone of the civil rights movement in the United States. Anyone alive at that time will not forget the lines of marchers, arms linked, singing "We Shall Overcome" as they walked steadily toward the police who were massed to stop them. Music binds together people who might individually be terrified but who collectively become powerful advocates for themselves and others. Along with language, dancing, marching, and singing are uniquely human ways to install a sense of hope and courage.

I observed the force of communal rhythms in action when I watched Archbishop Desmond Tutu conduct public hearings for the Truth and Reconciliation Commission in South Africa in 1996. These events were framed by collective singing and dancing. Witnesses recounted the unspeakable atrocities that had been inflicted on them and their families. When they became overwhelmed, Tutu would interrupt their testimony and lead the entire audience in prayer, song, and dance until the witnesses could contain their sobbing and halt their physical collapse. This enabled participants to pendulate in and out of reliving their horror and eventually to find words to describe what had happened to them. I fully credit Tutu and the other member of the commission with averting what might have been an orgy of revenge, as is so common when victims are finally set free.

A few years ago I discovered *Keeping Together in Time*,[4] written by the great historian William H. McNeill near the end of his career. This short book examines the historical role of dance and military drill in creating what McNeill calls "muscular bonding" and sheds a new light on the importance of theater, communal dance, and movement. It also solved a long-standing puzzle in my own mind. Having been raised in the Netherlands, I had always wondered how a group of simple Dutch peasants and fishermen had won their liberation from the mighty Spanish empire. The Eighty Years' War, which lasted from the late sixteenth to the midseventeenth century, began as a series of guerrilla actions, and it seemed destined to remain that way, since the ill-disciplined, ill-paid soldiers regularly fled under volleys of musket fire.

This changed when Prince Maurice of Orange became the leader of the Dutch rebels. Still in his early twenties, he had recently completed his schooling in Latin, which enabled him to read 1,500-year-old Roman manuals on military tactics. He learned that the Roman general Lycurgus had introduced marching in step to the Roman legions and that the historian Plutarch had attributed their invincibility to this practice: "It was at once a magnificent and terrible sight, to see them march on to the tune of their flutes, without any disorder in their ranks, any discomposure in their minds or change in their countenances, calmly and cheerfully moving with music to the deadly fight."[5]

Prince Maurice instituted close-order drill, accompanied by drums, flutes, and trumpets, in his ragtag army. This collective ritual not only provided his men with a sense of purpose and solidarity, but also made it possible for them to execute complicated maneuvers. Close-order drill subsequently spread across Europe, and to this day the major services of the U.S. military spend liberally on their marching bands, even though fifes and drums no longer accompany troops into battle.

Neuroscientist Jaak Panksepp, who was born in the tiny Baltic country of Estonia, told me the remarkable story of Estonia's "Singing Revolution." In June 1987, on one of those endless sub-Arctic summer evenings, more than ten thousand concertgoers at the Tallinn Song Festival Grounds linked hands and began to sing patriotic songs that had been forbidden during half a century of Soviet occupation. These songfests and protests continued, and on September 11, 1988, three hundred thousand people, about a quarter of the population of Estonia, gathered to sing and make a public demand for independence. By August 1991 the Congress of Estonia had proclaimed the restoration of the Estonian state, and when Soviet tanks attempted to intervene, people acted as human shields to protect Tallinn's radio and TV stations. As a columnist noted in the *New York Times*: "Imagine the scene in *Casablanca* in which the French patrons sing "La Marseillaise" in defiance of the Germans, then multiply its power by a factor of thousands, and you've only begun to imagine the force of the Singing Revolution."[6]

TREATING TRAUMA THROUGH THEATER

It is surprising how little research exists on how collective ceremonies affect the mind and brain and how they might prevent or alleviate trauma. Over the past decade, however, I have had a chance to observe and study three different programs for treating trauma through theater: Urban Improv in Boston[7] and the Trauma Drama program it inspired in the Boston public schools and in our residential centers;[8] the Possibility Project, directed by Paul Griffin in New York City;[9] and Shakespeare & Company, in Lenox, Massachusetts, which runs a program for juvenile offenders called Shakespeare in the Courts.[10] In this chapter, I'll focus on these three groups, but there are many excellent therapeutic drama programs in the United States and abroad, making theater a widely available resource for recovery.

Despite their differences, all of these programs share a common foundation: confrontation of the painful realities of life and symbolic transformation through communal action. Love and hate, aggression and surrender, loyalty and betrayal are the stuff of theater and the stuff of trauma. As a culture we are trained to cut ourselves off from the truth of what we're feeling. In the words of Tina Packer, the charismatic founder of Shakespeare & Company: "Training actors involves training people to go against that tendency—not only to feel deeply, but to convey that feeling at every moment to the audience, so the audience will get it —and not close off against it."

Traumatized people are terrified to feel deeply. They are afraid to experience their emotions, because emotions lead to loss of control. In contrast, theater is about embodying emotions, giving voice to them, becoming rhythmically engaged, taking on and embodying different roles.

As we've seen, the essence of trauma is feeling godforsaken, cut off from the human race. Theater involves a collective confrontation with the realities of the human condition. As Paul Griffin, discussing his theater program for foster-care children, told me: "The stuff of tragedy in theater revolves around coping with betrayal, assault, and destruction. These kids have no trouble understanding what Lear, Othello, Macbeth, or Hamlet are all about." In Tina Packer's words: "Everything is about using the whole body and having other bodies resonate with your feelings, emotions and thoughts." Theater gives trauma survivors a chance to connect with one another by deeply experiencing their common humanity.

Traumatized people are afraid of conflict. They fear losing control and ending up on the losing side once again. Conflict is central to theater—inner conflicts, interpersonal conflicts, family conflicts, social conflicts, and their consequences. Trauma is about trying to forget, hiding how scared, enraged, or helpless you are. Theater is about finding ways of telling the truth and conveying deep truths to your audience. This requires pushing through blockages to discover your own truth, exploring and examining your own internal experience so that it can emerge in your voice and body on stage.

MAKING IT SAFE TO ENGAGE

These theater programs are not for aspiring actors but for angry, frightened, and obstreperous teenagers or withdrawn, alcoholic, burned-out veterans. When they come to rehearsal, they slump into their chairs, fearful that others will immediately see what failures they are. Traumatized adolescents are a jumble: inhibited, out of tune, inarticulate, uncoordinated, and purposeless. They are too hyperaroused to notice what is going on around them. They are easily triggered and rely on action rather than words to discharge their feelings.

All the directors I've worked with agree that the secret is to go slow and engage them bit by bit. The initial challenge is simply to get participants to be more present in the room. Here's Kevin Coleman, director of Shakespeare in the Courts, describing his work with teens when I interviewed him: "First we get them up and walking around the room. Then we start to create a balance in the space, so they're not walking aimlessly, but become aware of other people. Gradually, with little prompts, it becomes more complex: Just walk on your toes, or on your heels, or walk backwards. Then, when you bump into someone, scream and fall down. After maybe thirty prompts, they're out there waving their arms in the air, and we get to a full-body warm up, but it's incremental. If you take too big a jump, you'll see them hit the wall.

"You have to make it safe for them to notice each other. Once their bodies are a little more free, I might use the prompt: 'Don't make eye contact with anyone—just look at the floor.' Most of them are thinking: 'Great, I'm doing that already,' but then I say 'Now begin to notice people as you go by, but don't let them see you looking.' And next: 'Just make eye contact for a second.' Then: 'Now, no eye contact . . . now, contact . . . now, no contact. Now, make eye contact and *hold* it . . . too long. You'll know when it's too long because you'll either want to start dating that person or to have a fight with them. That's when it's too long.'

"They don't make that kind of extended eye contact in their normal lives, not even with a person they're talking to. They don't know if that person is safe or not. So what you're doing is making it safe for them not to disappear when they make eye contact, or when someone looks at them. Bit by bit, by bit, by bit . . ."

Traumatized adolescents are noticeably out of sync. In the Trauma Center's Trauma Drama program, we use mirroring exercises to help them to get in tune with one another. They move their right arm up, and their partner mirrors it; they twirl, and their partner twirls in response. They begin to observe how body movements and facial expressions change, how their own natural movements differ from those of others, and how unaccustomed movements and expressions make them feel. Mirroring loosens their preoccupation with what other people think of them and helps them attune viscerally, not cognitively, to someone else's experience. When mirroring ends in giggles, it's a sure indication that our participants feel safe.

In order to become real partners, they also need to learn to trust one another. An exercise in which one person is blindfolded while his partner leads him by the hand is especially tough for our kids. It's often as terrifying for them to be the leader, to be trusted by someone vulnerable, as it is to be blindfolded and led. At first they may last for only ten or twenty seconds, but we gradually work them up to five minutes. Afterward some of them have to go off by themselves for a while, because it is so emotionally overwhelming to feel these connections.

The traumatized kids and veterans we work with are embarrassed to be seen, afraid to be in touch with what they are feeling, and they keep one another at arm's length. The job of any director, like that of any therapist, is to slow things down so the actors can establish a relationship with themselves, with their bodies. Theater offers a unique way to access a full range of emotions and physical sensations that not only put them in touch with the habitual "set" of their bodies, but also let them explore alternative ways of engaging with life.

URBAN IMPROV

My son loved his theater group, which was run by Urban Improv (UI), a long-standing Boston arts institution. He stayed with them through high school and then volunteered to work with them the summer after his freshman year in college. It was then that he learned that UI's violence prevention program, which has run hundreds of workshops in local schools since 1992, had received a research grant to assess its efficacy—and that they were looking for someone to head the study. Nick suggested to the directors, Kippy Dewey and Cissa Campion, that his dad would be the ideal person for the job. Luckily for me, they agreed.

I began to visit schools with UI's multicultural ensemble, which included a director, four professional actor-educators, and a musician. Urban Improv creates scripted skits depicting the kinds of problems that students face every day: exclusion from peer groups, jealousy, rivalry and anger, and family strife. Skits for older students also address issues like dating, STDs, homophobia, and peer violence. In a typical presentation the professional actors might portray a group of kids excluding a newcomer from a lunch table in the cafeteria. As the scene approaches a choice point—for example, the new student responds to their put-downs—the director freezes the action. A member of the class is then invited to replace one of the actors and show how he or she would feel and behave in this situation. These scenarios enable the students to observe day-to-day problems with some emotional distance while experimenting with various solutions: Will they confront the tormenters, talk to a friend, call the homeroom teacher, tell their parents what happened?

Another volunteer is then asked to try a different approach, so that students can see how other choices might play out. Props and costumes help the participants take risks in new roles, as do the playful atmosphere and the support from the actors. In the discussion groups afterward students respond to questions like "How was this scene similar or different from what happens in your school?" "How do you get the respect that you need?" and "How do you settle your differences?" These discussions become lively exchanges as many students volunteer their thoughts and ideas.

Our Trauma Center team evaluated this program at two grade levels in seventeen participating schools. Classrooms that participated in the UI program were compared with similar nonparticipating classrooms. At the fourth-grade level, we found a significant positive response. On standardized rating scales for aggression, cooperation, and self-control, students in the UI group showed substantially fewer fights and angry outbursts, more cooperation and self-assertion with peers, and more attentiveness and engagement in the classroom.[11]

Much to our surprise, these results were not matched by the eighth graders. What had happened in the interim that affected their responses? At first we had only our personal impressions to go on. When I'd visited the fourth-grade classes, I'd been struck by their wide-eyed innocence and their eagerness to participate. The eighth graders, in contrast, were often sullen and defensive and as a group seemed to have lost their spontaneity and enthusiasm. Onset of puberty was one obvious factor for the change, but might there be others?

When we delved further, we found that the older children had experienced more than twice as much trauma as the younger ones: Every single eighth grader in these typical American inner-city schools had witnessed serious violence. Two-thirds had observed five or more incidents, including stabbings, gunfights, killings, and domestic assaults. Our data showed that eighth graders with such high levels of exposure to violence were significantly more aggressive than students without these histories and that the program made no significant difference in their behavior.

The Trauma Center team decided to see if we could turn this situation around with a longer and more intensive program that focused on team building and emotion-regulation exercises, using scripts that dealt directly with the kinds of violence these kids experienced. For several months members of our staff, led by Joseph Spinazzola, met weekly with the UI actors to work on script development. The actors taught our psychologists improvisation, mirroring, and precise physical attunement so they could credibly portray melting down, confronting, cowering, or collapsing. We taught the actors about trauma triggers and how to recognize and deal with trauma reenactments.[12]

During the winter and spring of 2005, we tested the resulting program at a specialized day school run jointly by the Boston Public Schools and the Massachusetts Department of Correction. This was a chaotic environment in which students often shuttled back and forth between school and jail. All of them came from high-crime neighborhoods and had been exposed to horrendous violence; I had never seen such an aggressive and sullen group of kids. We got a glimpse into the lives of the innumerable middle school and high school teachers who deal daily with students whose first response to new challenges is to lash out or go into defiant withdrawal.

We were shocked to discover that, in scenes where someone was in physical danger, the students always sided with the aggressors. Because they could not tolerate any sign of weakness in themselves, they could not accept it in others. They showed nothing but contempt for potential victims, yelling things like, "Kill the bitch, she deserves it," during a skit about dating violence.

At first some of the professional actors wanted to give up—it was simply too painful to see how mean these kids were—but they stuck it out, and I was amazed to see how they gradually got the students to experiment, however reluctantly, with new roles. Toward the end of the program, a few students were even volunteering for parts that involved showing vulnerability or fear. When they received their certificate of completion, several shyly gave the actors drawings to express their appreciation. I detected a few tears, possibly even in myself.

Our attempt to make Trauma Drama a regular part of the eighth-grade curriculum in the Boston public schools unfortunately ran into a wall of bureaucratic resistance. Nonetheless, it lives on as an integral part of the residential treatment programs at the Justice Resource Institute, while music, theater, art, and sports—timeless ways of fostering competence and collective bonding—continue to disappear from our schools.

THE POSSIBILITY PROJECT

In Paul Griffin's New York City Possibility Project the actors are not presented with prepared scripts. Instead, over a nine-month period they meet for three hours a week, write their own full-length musical, and perform it for several hundred people. During its twenty-year history the Possibility Project has accrued a stable staff and strong traditions. Each production team is made up of recent graduates who, with the help of professional actors, dancers, and musicians, organize scriptwriting, scenic design, choreography, and rehearsals for the incoming class. These recent grads are powerful role models. As Paul told me: "When they come into the program, students believe they cannot make a difference; putting a program like this together is a transforming experience for their future."

In 2010 Paul started a new program specifically for foster-care youth. This is a troubled population: Five years after maturing out of care, some 60 percent will have been convicted of a crime, 75 percent will be on public assistance, and only 6 percent will have completed even a community college degree.

The Trauma Center treats many foster care kids, but Griffin gave me a new way to see their lives: "Understanding foster care is like learning about a foreign country. If you're not from there, you don't speak the language. Life is upside down for foster-care youth." The security and love that other children take for granted they have to create for themselves. When Griffin says, "Life is upside down," he means that if you treat kids in foster care with love or generosity, they often don't know what to make of it or how to respond. Rudeness feels more familiar; cynicism they understand.

As Griffin points out, "Abandonment makes it impossible to trust, and kids who have gone through foster care understand abandonment. You can have no impact until they trust you." Foster-care children often answer to multiple people in charge. If they want to switch schools, for example, they have to deal with foster parents, school officials, the foster-care agency, and sometimes a judge. This tends to make them politically savvy, and they learn all too well how to play people.

In the foster-care world, "permanency" is a big buzzword. The motto is "One caring adult—that's all you need." However, it is natural for teenagers to pull away from adults, and Griffin remarks that the best form of permanency for teens is a steady group of friends—which the program is designed to provide. Another foster-care buzzword is "independence," which Paul counters with "*inter*dependence." "We're all interdependent," he points out. "The idea that we're asking our young people to go out in the world completely alone and call themselves independent is crazy. We need to teach them how to be interdependent, which means teaching them how to have relationships."

Paul found that foster-care youth are natural actors. Playing tragic characters, you have to express emotions and create a reality that comes from a place of depth and sorrow and hurt. Young people in foster care? That's all they know. It's life and death every day for them. Over time, collaboration helps the kids become important people in one another's lives. Phase one of the program is group building. The first rehearsal establishes basic agreements: responsibility, accountability, respect; yes to expressions of affection, no to sexual contact in the group. They then begin singing and moving together, which gets them in sync.

Now comes phase two: sharing life stories. They are now listening to one another, discovering shared experiences, breaking through the loneliness and isolation of trauma. Paul gave me a film that shows how this happened in one group. When the kids are first asked to say or do something to introduce themselves, they freeze, their faces expressionless, their eyes cast down, doing anything they can to become invisible.

As they begin to talk, as they discover a voice in which they themselves are central, they also begin to create their own show. Paul makes it clear the production depends on their input: "If you could write a musical or play, what would you put in it? Punishment? Revenge? Betrayal? Loss? This is your show to write." Everything they say is written down, and some of them start to put their own words on paper. As a script emerges, the production team incorporates the students' precise words into the songs and dialogue. The group will learn that if they can embody their experiences well enough, other people will listen. They will learn to feel what they feel and know what they know.

The focus changes naturally as rehearsals begin. The foster kids' history of pain, alienation, and fear is no longer central, and the emphasis shifts to "How can I become the best actor, singer, dancer, choreographer, or lighting and set designer I can possibly be?" Being able to perform becomes the critical issue: Competence is the best defense against the helplessness of trauma.

This is, of course, true for all of us. When the job goes bad, when a cherished project fails, when someone you count on leaves you or dies, there are few things as helpful as moving your muscles and doing something that demands focused attention. Inner-city schools and psychiatric programs often lose sight of this. They want the kids to behave "normally"—without building the competencies that will make them feel normal.

Theater programs also teach cause and effect. A foster kid's life is completely unpredictable. Anything can happen without notice: being triggered and having a meltdown; seeing a parent arrested or killed; being moved from one home to another; getting yelled at for things that got you approval in your last placement. In a theatrical production they see the consequences of their decisions and actions laid out directly before their eyes. "If you want to give them a sense of control, you have to give them power over their destiny rather than intervene on their behalf," Paul explains. "You cannot help, fix, or save the young people you are working with. What you can do is work side by side with them, help them to understand their vision, and realize it with them. By doing that you give them back control. We're healing trauma without anyone ever mentioning the word."

SENTENCED TO SHAKESPEARE

For the teenagers attending sessions of Shakespeare in the Courts, there is no improvisation, no building scripts around their own lives. They are all "adjudicated offenders" found guilty of fighting, drinking, stealing, and property crimes, and a Berkshire County Juvenile Court judge has sentenced them to six weeks, four afternoons a week, of intensive acting study. Shakespeare is a foreign country for these actors. As Kevin Coleman told me, when they first turn up—angry, suspicious, and in shock—they're convinced that they'd rather go to jail. Instead they're going to learn the lines of Hamlet, or Mark Antony, or Henry V and then go onstage in a condensed performance of an entire Shakespeare play before an audience of family, friends, and representatives of the juvenile justice system.

With no words to express the effects of their capricious upbringing, these adolescents act out their emotions with violence. Shakespeare calls for sword fighting, which, like other martial arts, gives them an opportunity to practice contained aggression and expressions of physical power. The emphasis is on keeping everyone safe. The kids love swordplay, but to keep one another safe they have to negotiate and use language.

Shakespeare was writing at a time of transition, when the world was moving from primarily oral to written communication—when most people were still signing their name with an *X*. These kids are facing their own period of transition; many are barely articulate, and some struggle to read at all. If they rely on four-letter words, it's not only to show they're tough but because they have no other language to communicate who they are or what they feel. When they discover the richness and the potential of language, they often have a visceral experience of joy.

The actors first investigate what, exactly, Shakespeare is saying, line by line. The director feeds the words one by one into the actors' ears, and they are instructed to say the line on the outgoing breath. At the beginning of the process, many of these kids can barely get a line out. Progress is slow, as each actor slowly internalizes the words. The words gain depth and resonance as the voice changes in response to their associations. The idea is to inspire the actors to sense their reactions to the words—and so to discover the character. Rather than "I have to remember my lines," the emphasis is on "What do these words mean to *me*? What effect do *I* have on my fellow actors? And what happens to me when I hear their lines?"[13]

This can be a life-changing process, as I witnessed in a workshop run by actors trained by Shakespeare & Company at the VA Medical Center in Bath, New York. Larry, a fifty-nine-year-old Vietnam veteran with twenty-seven detox hospitalizations during the previous year, had volunteered to play the role of Brutus in a scene from *Julius Caesar*. As the rehearsal began, he mumbled and hurried through his lines; he seemed to be terrified of what people were thinking of him.

> *Remember March, the ides of March remember:*
> *Did not great Julius bleed for justice' sake?*
> *What villain touch'd his body, that did stab,*
> *And not for justice?*

It seemed to take hours to rehearse the speech that begins with these lines.

At first he was just standing there, shoulders slumped, repeating the words that the director whispered in his ear: "*Remember*—what do you remember? Do you remember too much? Or not enough? *Remember.* What don't you want to remember? What is it like to remember?" Larry's voice cracked, eyes to the floor, sweat beading on his forehead.

After a short break and a sip of water, back to work. "*Justice*—did you receive justice? Did you ever bleed for justice's sake? What does justice mean to you? *Struck.* Have you ever struck someone? Have you ever been struck? What was it like? What do you wish you had done? *Stab.* Have you ever stabbed someone? Have you ever felt stabbed in the back? Have you stabbed someone in the back?" At this point Larry bolted from the room.

The next day he returned and we began again—Larry standing there, perspiring, heart racing, having a million associations going through his mind, gradually allowing himself to feel every word and learning to own the lines that he uttered.

At the end of the program Larry started his first job in seven years, and he was still working the last I heard, six months later. Learning to experience and tolerate deep emotions is essential for recovery from trauma.

• • •

In Shakespeare in the Courts, the specificity of the language that is used in rehearsal extends to the students' offstage speech. Kevin Coleman notes that their talk is riddled with the expression "I feel like . . ." He goes on: "If you are confusing your emotional experiences with your judgments, your work becomes vague. If you ask them, 'How did that feel?' they'll immediately say: 'It felt good' or 'That felt bad.' Both of those are judgments. So we never say, 'How did that feel?' at the end of a scene, because it invites them to go to the judgment part of their brain."

Instead Coleman asks, "Did you notice any specific feelings that came up for you doing that scene?" That way they learn to name emotional experiences: "I felt angry when he said that." "I felt scared when he looked at me." Becoming embodied and, for lack of a better word, "en-languaged," helps the actors realize that they have many different emotions. The more they notice, the more curious they get.

When rehearsals begin, the kids have to learn to stand up straight and walk across a stage unselfconsciously. They have to learn to speak so that they can be heard in all parts of the theater, which in itself presents a huge challenge. The final performance means facing the community. The kids step out onto the stage, experiencing another level of vulnerability, danger, or safety, and they find out how much they can trust themselves. Gradually the eagerness to succeed, to show that they can do it, takes over. Kevin told me the story of a girl who played Ophelia in Hamlet. On the day of the performance he saw her waiting backstage, ready to go on, with a wastebasket clutched to her belly. (She explained that she was so nervous she was scared she'd throw up). She had been a chronic runaway from her foster homes and also from Shakespeare in the Courts. Because the program is committed to not throwing kids out if at all possible, the police and truant officers had repeatedly brought her back. There must have come a point when she began to realize that her role was essential to the group, or perhaps she sensed the intrinsic value of the experience for herself. At least for that day, she was choosing not to run.

THERAPY AND THEATER

I once heard Tina Packer declare to a roomful of trauma specialists: "Therapy and theater are intuition at work. They are the opposite of research, where one strives to step outside of one's own personal experience, even outside your patients' experience, to test the objective validity of assumptions. What makes therapy effective is deep, subjective resonance and that deep sense of truth and veracity that lives in the body." I am still hoping that someday we will prove Tina wrong and combine the rigor of scientific methods with the power of embodied intuition.

Edward, one of the Shakespeare & Company teachers, told me about an experience he'd had as a young actor in Packer's advanced training workshop. The group had spent the morning doing exercises aimed at getting the muscles of the torso to release, so that the breath could drop in naturally and fully. Edward noticed that every time he rolled through one section of his ribs, he'd feel a wave of sadness. The coach asked if he'd ever been injured there, and he said no.

For Packer's afternoon class he'd prepared a speech from *Richard II* where the king is summoned to give up his crown to the lord who has usurped him. During the discussion afterward, he recalled that his mother had broken her ribs when she was pregnant with him and that he'd always associated this with his premature birth.

As he recalled:

When I told Tina this, she started asking me questions about my first few months. I said I didn't remember being in an incubator but that I remembered times later when I stopped breathing, and being in the hospital in an oxygen tent. I remembered being in my uncle's car and him driving through red lights to get me to the emergency room. It was like having sudden infant death syndrome at the age of three.

Tina kept asking me questions, and I started to get really frustrated and angry at her poking away at whatever shield I had around that pain. Then she said, "Was it painful when the doctors stuck all those needles in you?"

At that moment, I just started screaming. I tried to leave the room, but two of the other actors—really big guys—held me down. They finally got me to sit in a chair, and I was trembling and shaking. Then Tina said, "You're your mother and you're going to do this speech. You're your mother and you're giving birth to yourself. And you're telling yourself that you're going to make it. You're not going to die. You must convince yourself. You must convince that little newborn that you're not going to die."

This became my intention with Richard's speech. When I first brought the speech to class, I told myself that I wanted to get the role right, not that something welling deep inside me needed to say these words. When finally it did, it became so clear that my baby was like Richard; I was not ready to give up my throne. It was like megatons of energy and tension just left my body. Pathways opened up for expression that had been blocked by this baby holding his breath and being so afraid that it was going to die.

The genius of Tina was in having me become my mother telling me I'd be okay. It was almost like going back and changing the story. Being reassured that someday I would feel safe enough to express my pain made it a precious part of my life.

That night I had the first orgasm I'd ever had in the presence of another person. And I know it's because I released something—some tension in my body—that allowed me to be more in the world.

EPILOGUE

CHOICES TO BE MADE

We are on the verge of becoming a trauma-conscious society. Almost every day one of my colleagues publishes another report on how trauma disrupts the workings of mind, brain, and body. The ACE study showed how early abuse devastates health and social functioning, while James Heckman won a Nobel Prize for demonstrating the vast savings produced by early intervention in the lives of children from poor and troubled families: more high school graduations, less criminality, increased employment, and decreased family and community violence. All over the world I meet people who take these data seriously and who work tirelessly to develop and apply more effective interventions, whether devoted teachers, social workers, doctors, therapists, nurses, philanthropists, theater directors, prison guards, police officers, or meditation coaches. If you have come this far with me in *The Body Keeps the Score*, you have also become part of this community.

Advances in neuroscience have given us a better understanding of how trauma changes brain development, self-regulation, and the capacity to stay focused and in tune with others. Sophisticated imaging techniques have identified the origins of PTSD in the brain, so that we now understand why traumatized people become disengaged, why they are bothered by sounds and lights, and why they may blow up or withdraw in response to the slightest provocation. We have learned how, throughout life, experiences change the structure and function of the brain—and even affect the genes we pass on to our children. Understanding many of the fundamental processes that underlie traumatic stress opens the door to an array of interventions that can bring the brain areas related to self-regulation, self-perception, and attention back online. We know not only how to treat trauma but also, increasingly, how to prevent it.

And yet, after attending another wake for a teenager who was killed in a drive-by shooting in the Blue Hill Avenue section of Boston or after reading about the latest school budget cuts in impoverished cities and towns, I find myself close to despair. In many ways we seem to be regressing, with measures like the callous congressional elimination of food stamps for kids whose parents are unemployed or in jail; with the stubborn opposition to universal health care in some quarters; with psychiatry's obtuse refusal to make connection between psychic suffering and social conditions; with the refusal to prohibit the sale or possession of weapons whose only purpose is to kill large numbers of human beings; and with our tolerance for incarcerating a huge segment of our population, wasting their lives as well as our resources.

Discussions of PTSD still tend to focus on recently returned soldiers, victims of terrorist bombings, or survivors of terrible accidents. But trauma remains a much larger public health issue, arguably the greatest threat to our national well-being. Since 2001 far more Americans have died at the hands of their partners or other family members than in the wars in Iraq and Afghanistan. American women are twice as likely to suffer domestic violence as breast cancer. The American Academy of Pediatrics estimates that firearms kill twice as many children as cancer does. All around Boston I see signs advertising the Jimmy Fund, which fights children's cancer, and for marches to fund research on breast cancer and leukemia, but we seem too embarrassed or discouraged to mount a massive effort to help children and adults learn to deal with the fear, rage, and collapse, the predictable consequences of having been traumatized.

When I give presentations on trauma and trauma treatment, participants sometimes ask me to leave out the politics and confine myself to talking about neuroscience and therapy. I wish I could separate trauma from politics, but as long as we continue to live in denial and treat only trauma while ignoring its origins, we are bound to fail. In today's world your ZIP code, even more than your genetic code, determines whether you will lead a safe and healthy life. People's income, family structure, housing, employment, and educational opportunities affect not only their risk of developing traumatic stress but also their access to effective help to address it. Poverty, unemployment, inferior schools, social isolation, widespread availability of guns, and substandard housing all are breeding grounds for trauma. Trauma breeds further trauma; hurt people hurt other people.

My most profound experience with healing from collective trauma was witnessing the work of the South African Truth and Reconciliation Commission, which was based on the central guiding principle of *Ubuntu*, a Xhosa word that denotes sharing what you have, as in "My humanity is inextricably bound up in yours." Ubuntu recognizes that true healing is impossible without recognition of our common humanity and our common destiny.

We are fundamentally social creatures—our brains are wired to foster working and playing together. Trauma devastates the social-engagement system and interferes with cooperation, nurturing, and the ability to function as a productive member of the clan. In this book we have seen how many mental health problems, from drug addiction to self-injurious behavior, start off as attempts to cope with emotions that became unbearable because of a lack of adequate human contact and support. Yet institutions that deal with traumatized children and adults all too often bypass the emotional-engagement system that is the foundation of who we are and instead focus narrowly on correcting "faulty thinking" and on suppressing unpleasant emotions and troublesome behaviors.

People can learn to control and change their behavior, but only if they feel safe enough to experiment with new solutions. The body keeps the score: If trauma is encoded in heartbreaking and gut-wrenching sensations, then our first priority is to help people move out of fight-or-flight states, reorganize their perception of danger, and manage relationships. Where traumatized children are concerned, the last things we should be cutting from school schedules are the activities that can do precisely that: chorus, physical education, recess, and anything else that involves movement, play, and other forms of joyful engagement.

As we've seen, my own profession often compounds, rather than alleviates, the problem. Many psychiatrists today work in assembly-line offices where they see patients they hardly know for fifteen minutes and then dole out pills to relieve pain, anxiety, or depression. Their message seems to be "Leave it to us to fix you; just be compliant and take these drugs and come back in three months— but be sure not to use alcohol or (illegal) drugs to relieve your problems." Such shortcuts in treatment make it impossible to develop self-care and self-leadership. One tragic example of this orientation is the rampant prescription of painkillers, which now kill more people each year in the United States than guns or car accidents.

Our increasing use of drugs to treat these conditions doesn't address the real issues: What are these patients trying to cope with? What are their internal or external resources? How do they calm themselves down? Do they have caring relationships with their bodies, and what do they do to cultivate a physical sense of power, vitality, and relaxation? Do they have dynamic interactions with other people? Who really knows them, loves them, and cares about them? Whom can they count on when they're scared, when their babies are ill, or when they are sick themselves? Are they members of a community, and do they play vital roles in the lives of the people around them? What specific skills do they need to focus, pay attention, and make choices? Do they have a sense of purpose? What are they good at? How can we help them feel in charge of their lives?

I like to believe that once our society truly focuses on the needs of children, all forms of social support for families—a policy that remains so controversial in this country—will gradually come to seem not only desirable but also doable. What difference would it make if all American children had access to high-quality day care where parents could safely leave their children as they went off to work or school? What would our school systems look like if all children could attend well-staffed preschools that cultivated cooperation, self-regulation, perseverance, and concentration (as opposed to focusing on passing tests, which will likely happen once children are allowed to follow their natural curiosity and desire to excel, and are not shut down by hopelessness, fear, and hyperarousal)?

I have a family photograph of myself as a five-year-old, perched between my older (obviously wiser) and younger (obviously more dependent) siblings. In the picture I proudly hold up a wooden toy boat, grinning from ear to ear: "See what a wonderful kid I am and see what an incredible boat I have! Wouldn't you love to come and play with me?" All of us, but especially children, need such confidence—confidence that others will know, affirm, and cherish us. Without that we can't develop a sense of agency that will enable us to assert: "This is what I believe in; this is what I stand for; this is what I will devote myself to." As long as we feel safely held in the hearts and minds of the people who love us, we will climb mountains and cross deserts and stay up all night to finish projects. Children and adults will do anything for people they trust and whose opinion they value.

But if we feel abandoned, worthless, or invisible, nothing seems to matter. Fear destroys curiosity and playfulness. In order to have a healthy society we must raise children who can safely play and learn. There can be no growth without curiosity and no adaptability without being able to explore, through trial and error, who you are and what matters to you. Currently more than 50 percent of the children served by Head Start have had three or more adverse childhood experiences like those included in the ACE study: incarcerated family members, depression, violence, abuse, or drug use in the home, or periods of homelessness.

People who feel safe and meaningfully connected with others have little reason to squander their lives doing drugs or staring numbly at television; they don't feel compelled to stuff themselves with carbohydrates or assault their fellow human beings. However, if nothing they do seems to make a difference, they feel trapped and become susceptible to the lure of pills, gang leaders, extremist religions, or violent political movements—anybody and anything that promises relief. As the ACE study has shown, child abuse and neglect is the single most preventable cause of mental illness, the single most common cause of drug and alcohol abuse, and a significant contributor to leading causes of death such as diabetes, heart disease, cancer, stroke, and suicide.

My colleagues and I focus much of our work where trauma has its greatest impact: on children and adolescents. Since we came together to establish the National Child Traumatic Stress Network in 2001, it has grown into a collaborative network of more than 150 centers nationwide, each of which has created programs in schools, juvenile justice systems, child welfare agencies, homeless shelters, military facilities, and residential group homes.

The Trauma Center is one of NCTSN's Treatment Development and Evaluation sites. My colleagues Joe Spinazzola, Margaret Blaustein, and I have developed comprehensive programs for children and adolescents that we, with the help of trauma-savvy colleagues in Hartford, Chicago, Houston, San Francisco, Anchorage, Los Angeles, and New York, are now implementing. Our team selects a particular area of the country to work in every two years, relying on local contacts to identify organizations that are energetic, open, and well respected; these will eventually serve as new nodes for treatment dissemination. For example, I collaborated for one two-year period with colleagues in Missoula, Montana, to help develop a culturally sensitive trauma program on Blackfoot Indian reservations.

The greatest hope for traumatized, abused, and neglected children is to receive a good education in schools where they are seen and known, where they learn to regulate themselves, and where they can develop a sense of agency. At their best, schools can function as islands of safety in a chaotic world. They can teach children how their bodies and brains work and how they can understand and deal with their emotions. Schools can play a significant role in instilling the resilience necessary to deal with the traumas of neighborhoods or families. If parents are forced to work two jobs to eke out a living, or if they are too impaired, overwhelmed, or depressed to be attuned to the needs of their kids, schools by default have to be the places where children are taught self-leadership and an internal locus of control.

When our team arrives at a school, the teachers' initial response is often some version of "If I'd wanted to be a social worker, I would have gone to social work school. But I came here to be a teacher." Many of them have already learned the hard way, however, that they cannot teach if they have a classroom filled with students whose alarm bells are constantly going off. Even the most committed teachers and school systems often come to feel frustrated and ineffective because so many of their kids are too traumatized to learn. Focusing only on improving test scores won't make any difference if teachers can't effectively address the behavior problems of these students. The good news is that the basic principles of trauma-focused interventions can be translated into practical day-to-day routines and approaches that can transform the entire culture of a school.

Most teachers we work with are intrigued to learn that abused and neglected students are likely to interpret any deviation from routine as danger and that their extreme reactions usually are expressions of traumatic stress. Children who defy the rules are unlikely to be brought to reason by verbal reprimands or even suspension—a practice that has become epidemic in American schools. Teachers' perspectives begin to change when they realize that these kids' disturbing behaviors started out as frustrated attempts to communicate distress and as misguided attempts to survive.

More than anything else, being able to feel safe with other people defines mental health; safe connections are fundamental to meaningful and satisfying lives. The critical challenge in a classroom setting is to foster reciprocity: truly hearing and being heard; really seeing and being seen by other people. We try to teach everyone in a school community—office staff, principals, bus drivers, teachers, and cafeteria workers—to recognize and understand the effects of trauma on children and to focus on the importance of fostering safety, predictability, and being known and seen. We make certain that the children are greeted by name every morning and that teachers make face-to-face contact with each and every one of them. Just as in our workshops, group work, and theater programs, we always start the day with check-ins: taking the time to share what's on everybody's mind.

Many of the children we work with have never been able to communicate successfully with language, as they are accustomed to adults who yell, command, sulk, or put earbuds in their ears. One of our first steps is to help their teachers model new ways of talking about feelings, stating expectations, and asking for help. Instead of yelling, "Stop!" when a child is throwing a tantrum or making her sit alone in the corner, teachers are encouraged to notice and name the child's experience, as in "I can see how upset you are"; to give her choices, as in "Would you like to go to the safe spot or sit on my lap?"; and to help her find words to describe her feelings and begin to find her voice, as in: "What will happen when you get home after class?" It may take many months for a child to know when it is safe to speak the truth (because it will never be universally safe), but for children, as for adults, identifying the truth of an experience is essential to healing from trauma.

It is standard practice in many schools to punish children for tantrums, spacing out, or aggressive outbursts—all of which are often symptoms of traumatic stress. When that happens, the school, instead of offering a safe haven, becomes yet another traumatic trigger. Angry confrontations and punishment can at best temporarily halt unacceptable behaviors, but since the underlying alarm system and stress hormones are not laid to rest, they are certain to erupt again at the next provocation.

In such situations the first step is acknowledging that a child is upset; then the teacher should calm him, then explore the cause and discuss possible solutions. For example, when a first-grader melts down, hitting his teacher and throwing objects around, we encourage his teacher to set clear limits while gently talking to him: "Would you like to wrap that blanket around you to help you calm down?" (The kid is likely to scream, "No!" but then curl up under the blanket and settle down.) Predictability and clarity of expectations are critical; consistency is essential. Children from chaotic backgrounds often have no idea how people can effectively work together, and inconsistency only promotes further confusion. Trauma-sensitive teachers soon realize that calling a parent about an obstreperous kid is likely to result in a beating and further traumatization.

Our goal in all these efforts is to translate brain science into everyday practice. For example, calming down enough to take charge of ourselves requires activating the brain areas that notice our inner sensations, the self-observing watchtower discussed in chapter 4. So a teacher might say: "Shall we take some deep breaths or use the breathing star?" (This is a colorful breathing aid made out of file folders.) Another option might be having the child sit in a corner wrapped in a heavy blanket while listening to some soothing music through headphones. Safe areas can help kids calm down by providing stimulating sensory awareness: the texture of burlap or velvet; shoe boxes filled with soft brushes and flexible toys. When the child is ready to talk again, he is encouraged to tell someone what is going on before he rejoins the group.

Kids as young as three can blow soap bubbles and learn that when they slow down their breathing to six breaths per minute and focus on the out breath as it flows over their upper lip, they will feel more calm and focused. Our team of yoga teachers works with children nearing adolescence specifically to help them "befriend" their bodies and deal with disruptive physical sensations. We know that one of the prime reasons for habitual drug use in teens is that they cannot stand the physical sensations that signal fear, rage, and helplessness.

Self-regulation can be taught to many kids who cycle between frantic activity and immobility. In addition to reading, writing, and arithmetic, all kids need to learn self-awareness, self-regulation, and communication as part of their core curriculum. Just as we teach history and geography, we need to teach children how their brains and bodies work. For adults and children alike, being in control of ourselves requires becoming familiar with our inner world and accurately identifying what scares, upsets, or delights us.

Emotional intelligence starts with labeling your own feelings and attuning to the emotions of the people around you. We begin very simply: with mirrors. Looking into a mirror helps kids to be aware of what they look like when they are sad, angry, bored, or disappointed. Then we ask them, "How do you feel when you see a face like that?" We teach them how their brains are built, what emotions are for, and where they are registered in their bodies, and how they can communicate their feelings to the people around them. They learn that their facial muscles give clues about what they are feeling and then experiment with how their facial expressions affect other people.

We also strengthen the brain's watchtower by teaching them to recognize and name their physical sensations. For example, when their chest tightens, that probably means that they are nervous; their breathing becomes shallow and they feel uptight. What does anger feel like, and what can they do to change that sensation in their body? What happens if they take a deep breath or take time out to jump rope or hit a punching bag? Does tapping acupressure points help? We try to provide children, teachers, and other care providers with a toolbox of ways to take charge of their emotional reactions.

To promote reciprocity, we use other mirroring exercises, which are the foundation of safe interpersonal communication. Kids practice imitating one another's facial expressions. They proceed to imitating gestures and sounds and then get up and move in sync. To play well, they have to pay attention to really seeing and hearing one another. Games like Simon Says lead to lots of sniggering and giggling—signs of safety and relaxation. When teenagers balk at these "stupid games," we nod understandingly and enlist their cooperation by asking them to demonstrate games to the little kids, who "need their help."

Teachers and leaders learn that an activity as simple as trying to keep a beach ball in the air as long as possible helps groups become more focused, cohesive, and fun. These are inexpensive interventions. For older children some schools have installed workstations costing less than two hundred dollars where students can play computer games to help them focus and to improve their heart rate variability (HRV) (discussed in chapter 16), just as we do in our own clinic.

Children and adults alike need to experience how rewarding it is to work at the edge of their abilities. Resilience is the product of agency: knowing that what you do can make a difference. Many of us remember what playing team sports, singing in the school choir, or playing in the marching band meant to us, especially if we had coaches or directors who believed in us, pushed us to excel, and taught us we could be better than we thought was possible. The children we reach need this experience.

Athletics, playing music, dancing, and theatrical performances all promote agency and community. They also engage kids in novel challenges and unaccustomed roles. In a devastated postindustrial New England town, my friends Carolyn and Eli Newberger are teaching El Sistema, an orchestral music program that originated in Venezuela. Several of my students run an after-school program in Brazilian *capoeira* in a high-crime area of Boston, and my colleagues at the Trauma Center continue the Trauma Drama program. Last year I spent three weeks helping two boys prepare a scene from *Julius Caesar*. An effeminate, shy boy was playing Brutus and had to summon up his full force to put down Cassius, played by the class bully, who had to be coached to play a corrupt general begging for mercy. The scene came to life only after the bully talked about his father's violence and his own vow never to show weakness to anyone. (Most bullies have themselves been bullied, and they despise kids who remind them of their own vulnerability.) Brutus's powerful voice, on the other hand, emerged after he realized that he'd made himself invisible to deal with his own family violence.

These intense communal efforts force kids to collaborate, compromise, and stay focused on the task at hand. Tensions often run high, but the kids stick with it because they want to earn the respect of their coaches or directors and don't want to let down the team—all feelings that are opposite to the vulnerability of being subjected to arbitrary abuse, the invisibility of neglect, and the godforsaken isolation of trauma.

Our NCTSN programs are working: Kids become less anxious and emotionally reactive and are less aggressive or withdrawn; they get along better and their school performance improves; their attention deficit, hyperactivity, and "oppositional defiant" problems decrease; and parents report that their children are sleeping better. Terrible things still happen to them and around them, but they are now able to talk about these events; they have built up the trust and resources to seek the help they need. Interventions are successful if they draw on our natural wellsprings of cooperation and on our inborn responses to safety, reciprocity, and imagination.

Trauma constantly confronts us with our fragility and with man's inhumanity to man but also with our extraordinary resilience. I have been able to do this work for so long because it drew me to explore our sources of joy, creativity, meaning, and connection—all the things that make life worth living. I can't begin to imagine how I would have coped with what many of my patients have endured, and I see their symptoms as part of their strength—the ways they learned to survive. And despite all their suffering many have gone on to become loving partners and parents, exemplary teachers, nurses, scientists, and artists.

Most great instigators of social change have intimate personal knowledge of trauma. Oprah Winfrey comes to mind, as do Maya Angelou, Nelson Mandela, and Elie Wiesel. Read the life history of any visionary, and you will find insights and passions that came from having dealt with devastation.

The same is true of societies. Many of our most profound advances grew out of experiencing trauma: the abolition of slavery from the Civil War, Social Security in response to the Great Depression, and the GI Bill, which produced our once vast and prosperous middle class, from World War II. Trauma is now our most urgent public health issue, and we have the knowledge necessary to respond effectively. The choice is ours to act on what we know.

ACKNOWLEDGMENTS

This book is the fruit of thirty years of trying to understand how people deal with, survive, and heal from traumatic experiences. Thirty years of clinical work with traumatized men, women and children; innumerable discussions with colleagues and students, and participation in the evolving science about how mind, brain, and body deal with, and recover from, overwhelming experiences.

Let me start with the people who helped me organize, and eventually publish, this book. Toni Burbank, my editor, with whom I communicated many times each week over a two-year period about the scope, organization, and specific contents of the book. Toni truly understood what this book is about, and that understanding has been critical in defining its form and substance. My agent, Brettne Bloom, understood the importance of this work, found a home for it with Viking, and provided critical support at critical moments. Rick Kot, my editor at Viking, supplied invaluable feedback and editorial guidance.

My colleagues and students at the Trauma Center have provided the feeding ground, laboratory, and support system for this work. They also have been constant reminders of the sober reality of our work for these three decades. I cannot name them all, but Joseph Spinazzola, Margaret Blaustein, Roslin Moore, Richard Jacobs, Liz Warner, Wendy D'Andrea, Jim Hopper, Fran Grossman, Alex Cook, Marla Zucker, Kevin Becker, David Emerson, Steve Gross, Dana Moore, Robert Macy, Liz Rice-Smith, Patty Levin, Nina Murray, Mark Gapen, Carrie Pekor, Debbie Korn, and Betta de Boer van der Kolk all have been critical collaborators. And of course Andy Pond and Susan Wayne of the Justice Resource Institute.

My most important companions and guides in understanding and researching traumatic stress have been Alexander McFarlane, Onno van der Hart, Ruth Lanius and Paul Frewen, Rachel Yehuda, Stephen Porges, Glenn Saxe, Jaak Panksepp, Janet Osterman, Julian Ford, Brad Stolback, Frank Putnam, Bruce Perry, Judith Herman, Robert Pynoos, Berthold Gersons, Ellert

Nijenhuis, Annette Streeck-Fisher, Marylene Cloitre, Dan Siegel, Eli Newberger, Vincent Felitti, Robert Anda, and Martin Teicher; as well as my colleagues who taught me about attachment: Edward Tronick, Karlen Lyons-Ruth, and Beatrice Beebe.

Peter Levine, Pat Ogden, and Al Pesso read my paper on the importance of the body in traumatic stress back in 1994 and then offered to teach me about the body. I am still learning from them, and that learning has since then been expanded by yoga and meditation teachers Stephen Cope, Jon Kabat-Zinn, and Jack Kornfield.

Sebern Fisher first taught me about neurofeedback. Ed Hamlin and Larry Hirshberg later expanded that understanding. Richard Schwartz taught me internal family systems (IFS) therapy and assisted in helping to write the chapter on IFS. Kippy Dewey and Cissa Campion introduced me to theater, Tina Packer tried to teach me how to do it, and Andrew Borthwick-Leslie provided critical details.

Adam Cummings, Amy Sullivan, and Susan Miller provided indispensible support, without which many projects in this book could never have been accomplished.

Licia Sky created the environment that allowed me to concentrate on writing this book; she provided invaluable feedback on each one of the chapters; she donated her artistic gifts to many illustrations; and she contributed to sections on body awareness and clinical case material. My trusty secretary, Angela Lin, took care of multiple crises and kept the ship running at full speed. Ed and Edith Schonberg often provided a shelter from the storm; Barry and Lorrie Goldensohn served as literary critics and inspiration; and my children, Hana and Nicholas, showed me that every new generation lives in a world that is radically different from the previous one, and that each life is unique—a creative act by its owner that defies explanation by genetics, environment, or culture alone.

Finally, my patients, to whom I dedicate this book—I wish I could mention you all by name—who taught me almost everything I know—because you were my true textbook—and the affirmation of the life force, which drives us human beings to create a meaningful life, regardless of the obstacles we encounter.

APPENDIX

CONSENSUS PROPOSED CRITERIA FOR DEVELOPMENTAL TRAUMA DISORDER

The goal of introducing the diagnosis of Developmental Trauma Disorder is to capture the reality of the clinical presentations of children and adolescents exposed to chronic interpersonal trauma and thereby guide clinicians to develop and utilize effective interventions and for researchers to study the neurobiology and transmission of chronic interpersonal violence. Whether or not they exhibit symptoms of PTSD, children who have developed in the context of ongoing danger, maltreatment, and inadequate caregiving systems are ill-served by the current diagnostic system, as it frequently leads to no diagnosis, multiple unrelated diagnoses, an emphasis on behavioral control without recognition of interpersonal trauma and lack of safety in the etiology of symptoms, and a lack of attention to ameliorating the developmental disruptions that underlie the symptoms.

The Consensus Proposed Criteria for Developmental Trauma Disorder were devised and put forward in February 2009 by a National Child Traumatic Stress Network (NCTSN)-affiliated Task Force led by Bessel A. van der Kolk, MD and Robert S. Pynoos, MD, with the participation of Dante Cicchetti, PhD, Marylene Cloitre, PhD, Wendy D'Andrea, PhD, Julian D. Ford, PhD, Alicia F. Lieberman, PhD, Frank W. Putnam, MD, Glenn Saxe, MD, Joseph Spinazzola, PhD, Bradley C. Stolbach, PhD, and Martin Teicher, MD, PhD. The consensus proposed criteria are based on extensive review of empirical literature, expert clinical wisdom, surveys of NCTSN clinicians, and preliminary analysis of data from thousands of children in numerous clinical and child service system settings, including NCTSN treatment centers, state child welfare systems, inpatient psychiatric settings, and juvenile detention centers. Because their validity, prevalence, symptom thresholds, or clinical utility have yet to be examined through prospective data collection or analysis, these proposed criteria should not be viewed as a formal diagnostic category to be incorporated into the DSM as written here. Rather, they are intended to describe the most clinically significant symptoms exhibited by many children and adolescents following complex trauma. These proposed criteria have guided the Developmental Trauma Disorder field trials that began in 2009 and continue to this day.

CONSENSUS PROPOSED CRITERIA FOR DEVELOPMENTAL TRAUMA DISORDER

A. Exposure. The child or adolescent has experienced or witnessed multiple or prolonged adverse events over a period of at least one year beginning in childhood or early adolescence, including:

A. 1. Direct experience or witnessing of repeated and severe episodes of interpersonal violence; and

A. 2. Significant disruptions of protective caregiving as the result of repeated changes in primary caregiver; repeated separation from the primary caregiver; or exposure to severe and persistent emotional abuse

B. Affective and Physiological Dysregulation. The child exhibits impaired normative developmental competencies related to arousal regulation, including at least two of the following:

B. 1. Inability to modulate, tolerate, or recover from extreme affect states (e.g., fear, anger, shame), including prolonged and extreme tantrums, or immobilization

B. 2. Disturbances in regulation in bodily functions (e.g. persistent disturbances in sleeping, eating, and elimination; over-reactivity or under-reactivity to touch and sounds; disorganization during routine transitions)

B. 3. Diminished awareness/dissociation of sensations, emotions and bodily states

B. 4. Impaired capacity to describe emotions or bodily states

C. Attentional and Behavioral Dysregulation: The child exhibits impaired normative developmental competencies related to sustained attention, learning, or coping with stress, including at least three of the following:

C. 1. Preoccupation with threat, or impaired capacity to perceive threat, including misreading of safety and danger cues

C. 2. Impaired capacity for self-protection, including extreme risk-taking or thrill-seeking

C. 3. Maladaptive attempts at self-soothing (e.g., rocking and other rhythmical movements, compulsive masturbation)

C. 4. Habitual (intentional or automatic) or reactive self-harm

C. 5. Inability to initiate or sustain goal-directed behavior

D. Self and Relational Dysregulation. The child exhibits impaired normative developmental competencies in their sense of personal identity and involvement in relationships, including at least three of the following:

D. 1. Intense preoccupation with safety of the caregiver or other loved ones (including precocious caregiving) or difficulty tolerating reunion with them after separation

D. 2. Persistent negative sense of self, including self-loathing, helplessness, worthlessness, ineffectiveness, or defectiveness

D. 3. Extreme and persistent distrust, defiance or lack of reciprocal behavior in close relationships with adults or peers

D. 4. Reactive physical or verbal aggression toward peers, caregivers, or other adults

D. 5. Inappropriate (excessive or promiscuous) attempts to get intimate contact (including but not limited to sexual or physical intimacy) or excessive reliance on peers or adults for safety and reassurance

D. 6. Impaired capacity to regulate empathic arousal as evidenced by lack of empathy for, or intolerance of, expressions of distress of others, or excessive responsiveness to the distress of others

E. Posttraumatic Spectrum Symptoms. The child exhibits at least one symptom in at least two of the three PTSD symptom clusters B, C, & D.

F. Duration of disturbance (symptoms in DTD Criteria B, C, D, and E) at least 6 months.

G. Functional Impairment. The disturbance causes clinically significant distress or impairment in at least two of the following areas of functioning:

- Scholastic
- Familial
- Peer Group
- Legal
- Health
- Vocational (for youth involved in, seeking or referred for employment, volunteer work or job training)

B. A. van der Kolk, "Developmental Trauma Disorder: Toward A Rational Diagnosis For ChildrenWith Complex Trauma Histories," Psychiatric Annals, 35, no. 5 (2005): 401-408.

RESOURCES

- The Trauma Center at JRI. This is the website of the Trauma Center of which I am the medical director, which has numerous resources for special populations, various treatment approaches, lectures and courses: www.traumacenter.org.
- David Baldwin's Trauma Information Pages provide information for clinicians and researchers in the traumatic-stress field: http://www.trauma -pages.com/.
- National Child Traumatic Stress Network (NCTSN). Effective treatments for youth, trauma training, and education measures; reviews of measures examining trauma for parents, educators, judges, child welfare agencies, military personnel, and therapists: http://www.nctsnet.org/.
- American Psychological Association. Resource guide for traumatized people and their loved ones: http://www.apa.org/topics/trauma/.
- Averse Childhood Experiences. Several websites are devoted to the ACE study and its consequences: http://acestoohigh.com/got-your-ace-score/; http://www.cdc.gov/violenceprevention/acesstudy/; http://aces tudy.org/.
- Gift from Within PTSD Resources for Survivors and Caregivers: giftfromwithin.org.
- There & Back Again is a nonprofit organization that supports the well-being of service-members. Its mission is to provide reintegration support services to combat veterans of all conflicts: http://thereandbackagain.org/.
- HelpPRO Therapist Finder. Comprehensive listings of local therapists specializing in trauma and other concerns, serving specific

age groups, accepting payment options and more: http://www.helppro.com/.

- Sidran Foundation includes traumatic memories and general information about dealing with trauma: www.sidran.org.
- Traumatology. Green Cross Academy of Traumatology electronic journal, edited by Charles Figley: www.greencross.org/.
- PILOTS database at Dartmouth is a searchable database of the world's literature on post-traumatic stress disorder, produced by the National Center for PTSD: http://search.proquest.com/pilots/? accountid=28179.

GOVERNMENT RESOURCES

- National Center for PTSD includes links to the *PTSD Research Quarterly* and National Center divisions, including behavioral science division, clinical neuroscience division, and women's health sciences division: http://www.ptsd.va.gov/.
- Office for Victims of Crime in the Department of Justice. Provides a variety of resources for victims of crime in the United States and internationally, including the National Directory of Victim Assistance Funding Opportunities which lists, by state and territory, the contact names, mailing addresses, telephone numbers, and e-mail addresses for the federal grant programs that provide assistance to crime victims: http://ojp.gov/ovc/.
- National Institutes of Mental Health: http://www.nimh.nih.gov/health/topics/post-traumatic-stress-disorder-ptsd/index.shtml.

WEBSITES SPECIFICALLY DEALING WITH TRAUMA AND MEMORY

- Jim Hopper.com. Info on the stages of recovery, recovered memories, and comprehensive literature review on remembering trauma.
- The Recovered Memory Project. Archive compiled by Ross Cheit at Brown University: http://www.brown.edu/academics/taubman-center/.

MEDICATIONS

- About Medications for Combat PTSD. Jonathan Shay, MD, PhD, staff psychiatrist, Boston VA Outpatient Clinic: http://www.dr-bob.org/tips/ptsd.html. webMD http://www.webmd.com/drugs/condition=1020-post+traumatic+stress+disorderaspx? diseaseid=10200diseasename=post+traumatic+stress+disorder

PROFESSIONAL ORGANIZATIONS FOCUSED ON GENERAL TRAUMA RESEARCH AND DISSEMINATION

- International Society for Traumatic Stress Studies: www.istss.com.
- European Society for Traumatic Stress Studies: www.estss.org.
- International Society for the Study of Trauma and Dissociation (ISSTD): http://www.isst-d.org/.

PROFESSIONAL ORGANIZATIONS DEALING WITH PARTICULAR TREATMENT METHODS

- The EMDR International Association (EMDRIA): http://www.emdria.org/.
- Sensorimotor Institute (founded by Pat Ogden): http://www.sensorimotorpsychotherapy.org/home/index.html.
- Somatic experiencing (founded by Peter Levine): http://www.traumahealing.com/somatic-experiencing/index.html.
- Internal family systems therapy: http://www.selfleadership.org/.
- Pesso Boyden system psychomotor therapy: PBSP.com.

THEATER PROGRAMS (A SAMPLE OF PROGRAMS FOR TRAUMATIZED YOUTH)

- Urban Improv uses improvisational theater workshops to teach violence prevention, conflict resolution, and decision making: http://www.urbanimprov.org/.
- The Possibility Project. Based in NYC: http://the-possibility-project.org/.
- Shakespeare in the Courts: http://www.shakespeare.org/education/for-youth/shakespeare-courts/.

YOGA AND MINDFULNESS

- http://givebackyoga.org/.
- http://www.kripalu.org/.

- http://www.mindandlife.org/.

FURTHER READING

DEALING WITH TRAUMATIZED CHILDREN

- Blaustein, Margaret, and Kristine Kinniburgh. *Treating Traumatic Stress in Children and Adolescents: How to Foster Resilience through Attachment, Self-Regulation, and Competency.* New York: Guilford, 2012..
- Hughes, Daniel. *Building the Bonds of Attachment.* New York: Jason Aronson, 2006.
- Perry, Bruce, and Maia Szalavitz. *The Boy Who Was Raised as a Dog: And Other Stories from a Child Psychiatrist's Notebook.* New York: Basic Books, 2006.
- Terr, Lenore. *Too Scared to Cry: Psychic Trauma in Childhood.* Basic Books, 2008.
- Terr, Lenore C. *Working with Children to Heal Interpersonal Trauma: The Power of Play.* Ed., Eliana Gil. New York: Guilford Press, 2011.
- Saxe, Glenn, Heidi Ellis, and Julie Kaplow. *Collaborative Treatment of Traumatized Children and Teens: The Trauma Systems Therapy Approach.* New York: Guilford Press, 2006.
- Lieberman, Alicia, and Patricia van Horn. *Psychotherapy with Infants and Young Children: Repairing the Effects of Stress and Trauma on Early Attachment.* New York: Guilford Press, 2011.

PSYCHOTHERAPY

- Siegel, Daniel J. *Mindsight: The New Science of Personal Transformation.* New York: Norton, 2010.
- Fosha D., M. Solomon, and D. J. Siegel. *The Healing Power of*

Emotion: Affective Neuroscience, Development and Clinical Practice (Norton Series on Interpersonal Neurobiology). New York: Norton, 2009.

- Siegel, D., and M. Solomon: *Healing Trauma: Attachment, Mind, Body and Brain* (Norton Series on Interpersonal Neurobiology). New York: Norton, 2003.
- Courtois, Christine, and Julian Ford. *Treating Complex Traumatic Stress Disorders (Adults): Scientific Foundations and Therapeutic Models*. New York: Guilford, 2013.
- Herman, Judith. *Trauma and Recovery: The Aftermath of Violence—from Domestic Abuse to Political Terror*. New York: Basic Books, 1992.

NEUROSCIENCE OF TRAUMA

- Panksepp, Jaak, and Lucy Biven. *The Archaeology of Mind: Neuroevolutionary Origins of Human Emotions* (Norton Series on Interpersonal Neurobiology). New York: Norton, 2012.
- Davidson, Richard, and Sharon Begley. *The Emotional Life of Your Brain: How Its Unique Patterns Affect the Way You Think, Feel, and Live—and How You Can Change Them*. New York: Hachette, 2012.
- Porges, Stephen. *The Polyvagal Theory: Neurophysiological Foundations of Emotions, Attachment, Communication, and Self-regulation* (Norton Series on Interpersonal Neurobiology). New York: Norton, 2011.
- Fogel, Alan. *Body Sense: The Science and Practice of Embodied Self-Awareness* (Norton Series on Interpersonal Neurobiology). New York: Norton, 2009.
- Shore, Allan N. *Affect Regulation and the Origin of the Self: The Neurobiology of Emotional Development*. New York: Psychology Press, 1994.
- Damasio, Antonio R. *The Feeling of What Happens: Body and Emotion in the Making of Consciousness*. Houghton Mifflin Harcourt, 2000.

BODY-ORIENTED APPROACHES

- Cozzolino, Louis. *The Neuroscience of Psychotherapy: Healing the Social Brain*, second edition (Norton Series on Interpersonal Neurobiology). New York: Norton, 2010.
- Ogden, Pat, and Kekuni Minton. *Trauma and the Body: A Sensorimotor Approach to Psychotherapy* (Norton Series on Interpersonal Neurobiology). New York: Norton, 2008.
- Levine, Peter A. *In an Unspoken Voice: How the Body Releases Trauma and Restores Goodness*. Berkeley: North Atlantic, 2010.
- Levine, Peter A., and Ann Frederic. *Waking the Tiger: Healing Trauma*. Berkeley: North Atlantic, 2012
- Curran, Linda. *101 Trauma-Informed Interventions: Activities, Exercises and Assignments to Move the Client and Therapy Forward*. PESI, 2013.

EMDR

- Parnell, Laura. *Attachment-Focused EMDR: Healing Relational Trauma*. New York: Norton, 2013.
- Shapiro, Francine. *Getting Past Your Past: Take Control of Your Life with Self-Help Techniques from EMDR Therapy*. Emmaus, PA: Rodale, 2012.
- Shapiro, Francine, and Margot Silk Forrest. *EMDR: The Breakthrough "Eye Movement" Therapy for Overcoming Anxiety, Stress, and Trauma*. New York: Basic Books, 2004.

WORKING WITH DISSOCIATION

- Schwartz, Richard C. *Internal Family Systems Therapy* (The Guilford Family Therapy Series). New York: Guilford, 1997.
- O. van der Hart, E. R. Nijenhuis, and F. Steele. *The Haunted Self: Structural Dissociation and the Treatment of Chronic Traumatization*. New York: Norton, 2006.

COUPLES

- Gottman, John. *The Science of Trust: Emotional Attunement for Couples*. New York: Norton, 2011.

YOGA

- Emerson, David, and Elizabeth Hopper. *Overcoming Trauma through Yoga: Reclaiming Your Body.* Berkeley: North Atlantic, 2012.
- Cope, Stephen. *Yoga and the Quest for the True Self.* New York: Bantam Books, 1999.

NEUROFEEDBACK

- Fisher, Sebern. *Neurofeedback in the Treatment of Developmental Trauma: Calming the Fear-Driven Brain.* New York: Norton, 2014.
- Demos, John N. *Getting Started with Neurofeedback.* New York: Norton, 2005.
- Evans, James R. *Handbook of Neurofeedback: Dynamics and Clinical Applications.* CRC Press, 2013.

PHYSICAL EFFECTS OF TRAUMA

- Mate, Gabor *When the Body Says No: Understanding the Stress-Disease Connection.* New York: Random House, 2011.
- Sapolsky, Robert. *Why Zebras Don't Get Ulcers: The Acclaimed Guide to Stress, Stress-Related Diseases, and Coping.* New York: Macmillan 2004.

MEDITATION AND MINDFULNESS

- Zinn, Jon Kabat and Thich Nat Hanh. *Full Catastrophe Living: Using the Wisdom of Your Body and Mind to Face Stress, Pain, and Illness,* revised edition. New York: Random House, 2009.
- Kornfield, Jack. *A Path with Heart: A Guide Through The Perils and Promises of Spiritual Life.* New York: Random House, 2009.
- Goldstein, Joseph, and Jack Kornfield. *Seeking the Heart of Wisdom: The Path of Insight Meditation.* Shambhala Publications, 2001.

PSYCHOMOTOR THERAPY

- Pesso, Albert, and John S. Crandell. *Moving Psychotherapy: Theory and Application of Pesso System-Psychomotor Therapy.* Brookline Books, 1991.

- Pesso, Albert. *Experience In Action: A Psychomotor Psychology,* New York: New York University Press, 1969.

NOTES

PROLOGUE

1. V. Felitti, *et al.* "Relationship of Childhood Abuse and Household Dysfunction to Many of the Leading Causes of Death in Adults: The Adverse Childhood Experiences (ACE) Study." *American Journal of Preventive Medicine* 14, no. 4 (1998): 245–58.

CHAPTER 1: LESSONS FROM VIETNAM VETERANS

1. A. Kardiner, *The Traumatic Neuroses of War* (New York: P. Hoeber, 1941). Later I discovered that numerous textbooks on war trauma were published around both the First and Second World Wars, but as Abram Kardiner wrote in 1947: "The subject of neurotic disturbances consequent upon war has, in the past 25 years, been submitted to a good deal of capriciousness in public interest and psychiatric whims. The public does not sustain its interest, which was very great after World War I, and neither does psychiatry. Hence these conditions are not subject to continuous study."

2. Op cit, p. 7.

3. B. A. van der Kolk, "Adolescent Vulnerability to Post Traumatic Stress Disorder," *Psychiatry* 48 (1985): 365–70.

4. S. A. Haley, "When the Patient Reports Atrocities: Specific Treatment Considerations of the Vietnam Veteran," *Archives of General Psychiatry* 30 (1974): 191–96.

5. E. Hartmann, B. A. van der Kolk, and M. Olfield, "A Preliminary Study of the Personality of the Nightmare Sufferer," *American Journal of Psychiatry* 138 (1981): 794–97; B. A. van der Kolk, et al., "Nightmares and Trauma: Lifelong and Traumatic Nightmares in Veterans," *American Journal of Psychiatry* 141 (1984): 187–90.

6. B. A. van der Kolk and C. Ducey, "The Psychological Processing of Traumatic Experience: Rorschach Patterns in PTSD," *Journal of Traumatic Stress* 2 (1989): 259–74.

7. Unlike normal memories, traumatic memories are more like fragments of sensations, emotions, reactions, and images, that keep getting reexperienced in the present. The studies of Holocaust memories at Yale by Dori Laub and Nanette C. Auerhahn, as well as Lawrence L. Langer's book *Holocaust Testimonies: The Ruins of Memory*, and, most of all, Pierre Janet's 1889, 1893, and 1905 descriptions of the nature of traumatic memories helped us organize what we saw. That work will be discussed in the memory chapter.

8. D. J. Henderson, "Incest," in *Comprehensive Textbook of Psychiatry*, eds. A. M. Freedman and H. I. Kaplan, 2nd ed. (Baltimore: Williams & Wilkins, 1974), 1536.

9. Ibid.

10. K. H. Seal, et al., "Bringing the War Back Home: Mental Health Disorders Among 103,788 U.S. Veterans Returning from Iraq and Afghanistan Seen at Department of Veterans Affairs Facilities," *Archives of Internal Medicine* 167, no. 5 (2007): 476–82; C. W. Hoge, J. L. Auchterlonie, and C. S. Milliken, "Mental Health Problems, Use of Mental Health Services, and Attrition from Military Service After Returning from Deployment to Iraq or Afghanistan," *Journal of the American Medical Association* 295, no. 9 (2006): 1023–32.

11. D. G. Kilpatrick and B. E. Saunders, *Prevalence and Consequences of Child Victimization: Results from the National Survey of Adolescents: Final Report* (Charleston, SC: National Crime Victims Research and Treatment Center, Department of Psychiatry and Behavioral Sciences, Medical University of South Carolina 1997).

12. U.S. Department of Health and Human Services, Administration on Children, Youth and Families, *Child Maltreatment 2007*, 2009. See also U.S. Department of Health and Human Services, Administration for Children and Families, Administration on Children, Youth and Families, Children's Bureau, *Child Maltreatment 2010*, 2011.

CHAPTER 2: REVOLUTIONS IN UNDERSTANDING MIND AND BRAIN

1. G. Ross Baker, et al., "The Canadian Adverse Events Study: The Incidence of Adverse Events among Hospital Patients in Canada," *Canadian Medical Association Journal* 170, no. 11 (2004): 1678–86; A. C. McFarlane, et al., "Posttraumatic Stress Disorder in a General Psychiatric Inpatient Population," *Journal of Traumatic Stress* 14, no. 4 (2001): 633–45; Kim T. Mueser, et al., "Trauma and Posttraumatic Stress Disorder in Severe Mental Illness," *Journal of Consulting and Clinical Psychology* 66, no. 3 (1998): 493; National Trauma Consortium, www.nationaltraumaconsortium.org.

2. E. Bleuler, *Dementia Praecox or the Group of Schizophrenias*, trans. J. Zinkin (*Washington, DC*: International Universities Press, 1950), p. 227.

3. L. Grinspoon, J. Ewalt, and R. I. Shader, "Psychotherapy and Pharmacotherapy in Chronic Schizophrenia," *American Journal of Psychiatry* 124, no. 12 (1968): 1645–52. See also L. Grinspoon, J. Ewalt, and R. I. Shader, *Schizophrenia: Psychotherapy and Pharmacotherapy* (Baltimore: Williams and Wilkins, 1972).

4. T. R. Insel, "Neuroscience: Shining Light on Depression," *Science* 317, no. 5839 (2007): 757–58. See also C. M. France, P. H. Lysaker, and R. P. Robinson, "The 'Chemical Imbalance' Explanation for Depression: Origins, Lay Endorsement, and Clinical Implications," *Professional Psychology: Research and Practice* 38 (2007): 411–20.

5. B. J. Deacon, and J. J. Lickel, "On the Brain Disease Model of Mental Disorders," *Behavior Therapist* 32, no. 6 (2009).

6. J. O. Cole, et al., "Drug Trials in Persistent Dyskinesia (Clozapine)," in *Tardive Dyskinesia, Research and Treatment*, ed. R. C. Smith, J. M. Davis, and W. E. Fahn (New York: Plenum, 1979).

7. E. F. Torrey, *Out of the Shadows: Confronting America's Mental Illness Crisis* (New York: John Wiley & Sons, 1997). However, other factors were equally important, such as President Kennedy's 1963 Community Mental Health Act, in which the federal government took over paying for mental health care and which rewarded states for treating mentally ill people in the community.

8. American Psychiatric Association, Committee on Nomenclature. Work Group to Revise DSM-III. *Diagnostic and Statistical Manual of Mental Disorders* (American Psychiatric Publishing, 1980).

9. S. F. Maier and M. E. Seligman, "Learned Helplessness: Theory and Evidence," *Journal of Experimental Psychology: General* 105, no. 1 (1976): 3. See also M. E. Seligman, S. F. Maier, and J. H. Geer, "Alleviation of Learned Helplessness in the Dog," *Journal of Abnormal Psychology* 73, no. 3 (1968): 256; and R. L. Jackson, J. H. Alexander, and S. F. Maier, "Learned Helplessness, Inactivity, and Associative Deficits: Effects of Inescapable Shock on Response Choice Escape Learning," *Journal of Experimental Psychology: Animal Behavior Processes* 6, no. 1 (1980): 1.

10. G. A. Bradshaw and A. N. Schore, "How Elephants Are Opening Doors: Developmental Neuroethology, Attachment and Social Context," *Ethology* 113 (2007): 426–36.

11. D. Mitchell, S. Koleszar, and R. A. Scopatz, "Arousal and T-Maze Choice Behavior in Mice: A Convergent Paradigm for Neophobia Constructs and Optimal Arousal Theory," *Learning and Motivation* 15 (1984): 287–301. See also D. Mitchell, E. W. Osborne, and M. W. O'Boyle, "Habituation Under Stress: Shocked Mice Show Nonassociative Learning in a T-maze," *Behavioral and Neural Biology* 43 (1985): 212–17.

12. B. A. van der Kolk, et al., "Inescapable Shock, Neurotransmitters and Addiction to Trauma: Towards a Psychobiology of Post Traumatic Stress," *Biological Psychiatry* 20 (1985): 414–25.

13. C. Hedges, *War Is a Force That Gives Us Meaning* (New York: Random House Digital, 2003).

14. B. A. van der Kolk, "The Compulsion to Repeat Trauma: Revictimization, Attachment and Masochism," *Psychiatric Clinics of North America* 12 (1989): 389–411.

15. R. L. Solomon, "The Opponent-Process Theory of Acquired Motivation: The Costs of Pleasure and the Benefits of Pain," *American Psychologist* 35 (1980): 691–712.

16. H. K. Beecher, "Pain in Men Wounded in Battle," *Annals of Surgery* 123, no. 1 (January 1946): 96–105.

17. B. A. van der Kolk, et al., "Pain Perception and Endogenous Opioids in Post Traumatic Stress Disorder," *Psychopharmacology Bulletin* 25 (1989): 117–21. See also R. K. Pitman, et al., "Naloxone

Reversible Stress Induced Analgesia in Post Traumatic Stress Disorder," *Archives of General Psychiatry* 47 (1990): 541–47; and Solomon, "Opponent-Process Theory of Acquired Motivation."

18. J. A. Gray and N. McNaughton, "The Neuropsychology of Anxiety: Reprise," in *Nebraska Symposium on Motivation* (University of Nebraska Press, 1996), 43, 61–134. See also C. G. DeYoung and J. R. Gray, "Personality Neuroscience: Explaining Individual Differences in Affect, Behavior, and Cognition, in *The Cambridge Handbook of Personality Psychology (2009)*, 323–46.

19. M. J. Raleigh, et al., "Social and Environmental Influences on Blood Serotonin Concentrations in Monkeys," *Archives of General Psychiatry* 41 (1984): 505–10.

20. B. A. van der Kolk, et al., "Fluoxetine in Post Traumatic Stress," *Journal of Clinical Psychiatry* (1994): 517–22.

21. For the Rorschach aficionados among you, it reversed the C + CF/FC ratio.

22. Grace E. Jackson, *Rethinking Psychiatric Drugs: A Guide for Informed Consent* (AuthorHouse, 2005); Robert Whitaker, *Anatomy of an Epidemic: Magic Bullets, Psychiatric Drugs and the Astonishing Rise of Mental Illness in America* (New York: Random House, 2011).

23. We will return to this issue in chapter 15, where we discuss our study comparing Prozac with EMDR, in which EMDR had better long-term results than Prozac in treating depression, at least in adult onset trauma.

24. J. M. Zito, et al., "Psychotropic Practice Patterns for Youth: A 10-Year Perspective," *Archives of Pediatrics and Adolescent Medicine* 157 (January 2003): 17–25.

25. http://en.wikipedia.org/wiki/List_of_largest_selling_pharmaceutical_products.

26. Lucette Lagnado, "U.S. Probes Use of Antipsychotic Drugs on Children," *Wall Street Journal*, August 11, 2013.

27. Katie Thomas, "J.&J. to Pay $2.2 Billion in Risperdal Settlement," *New York Times*, November 4, 2013.

28. M. Olfson, et al., "Trends in Antipsychotic Drug Use by Very Young, Privately Insured Children," *Journal of the American Academy of Child & Adolescent Psychiatry* 49, no.1 (2010): 13–23.

29. M. Olfson, et al., "National Trends in the Outpatient Treatment of Children and Adolescents with Antipsychotic Drugs," *Archives of General Psychiatry* 63, no. 6 (2006): 679.

30. A. J. Hall, et al., "Patterns of Abuse Among Unintentional Pharmaceutical Overdose Fatalities," *Journal of the American Medical Association* 300, no. 22 (2008): 2613–20.

31. During the past decade two editors in chief of the most prestigious professional medical journal in the United States, the *New England Journal of Medicine*, Dr. Marcia Angell and Dr. Arnold Relman, have resigned from their positions because of the excessive power of the pharmaceutical industry over medical research, hospitals, and doctors. In a letter to the *New York Times* on December 28, 2004, Angell and Relman pointed out that the previous year one drug company had spent 28 percent of its revenues (more than $6 billion) on marketing and administrative expenses, while spending only half that on research and development; keeping 30 percent in net income was typical for the pharmaceutical industry. They concluded: "The medical profession should break its dependence on the pharmaceutical industry and educate its own." Unfortunately, this is about as likely as politicians breaking free from the donors that finance their election campaigns.

CHAPTER 3: LOOKING INTO THE BRAIN: THE NEUROSCIENCE REVOLUTION

1. B. Roozendaal, B. S. McEwen, and S. Chattarji, "Stress, Memory and the Amygdala," *Nature Reviews Neuroscience* 10, no. 6 (2009): 423–33.

2. R. Joseph, *The Right Brain and the Unconscious* (New York: Plenum Press, 1995).

3. The movie *The Assault* (based on the novel of the same name by Harry Mulisch), which won the Oscar for Best Foreign Language Film in 1986, is a good illustration of the power of deep early emotional impressions in determining powerful passions in adults.

4. This is the essence of cognitive behavioral therapy. See Foa, Friedman, and Keane, 2000 *Treatment*

Guidelines for PTSD.

CHAPTER 4: RUNNING FOR YOUR LIFE: THE ANATOMY OF SURVIVAL

1. R. Sperry, "Changing Priorities," *Annual Review of Neuroscience* 4 (1981): 1–15.
2. A. A. Lima, et al., "The Impact of Tonic Immobility Reaction on the Prognosis of Posttraumatic Stress Disorder," *Journal of Psychiatric Research* 44, no. 4 (March 2010): 224–28.
3. P. Janet, *L'automatisme psychologique* (Paris: Félix Alcan, 1889).
4. R. R. Llinás, *I of the Vortex: From Neurons to Self* (Cambridge, MA: MIT Press, 2002). See also R. Carter and C. D. Frith, *Mapping the Mind* (Berkeley: University of California Press, 1998); R. Carter, *The Human Brain Book* (Penguin, 2009); and J. J. Ratey, *A User's Guide to the Brain* (New York: Pantheon Books, 2001), 179.
5. B. D. Perry, et al., "Childhood Trauma, the Neurobiology of Adaptation, and Use Dependent Development of the Brain: How States Become Traits," *Infant Mental Health Journal* 16, no. 4 (1995): 271–91.
6. I am indebted to my late friend David Servan-Schreiber, who first made this distinction in his book *The Instinct to Heal.*
7. E. Goldberg, *The Executive Brain: Frontal Lobes and the Civilized Mind* (London, Oxford University Press, 2001).
8. G. Rizzolatti and L. Craighero "The Mirror-Neuron System," *Annual Review of Neuroscience* 27 (2004): 169–92. See also M. Iacoboni, et al., "Cortical Mechanisms of Human Imitation," *Science* 286, no. 5449 (1999): 2526–28; C. Keysers and V. Gazzola, "Social Neuroscience: Mirror Neurons Recorded in Humans," *Current Biology* 20, no. 8 (2010): R353–54; J. Decety and P. L. Jackson, "The Functional Architecture of Human Empathy," *Behavioral and Cognitive Neuroscience Reviews* 3 (2004): 71–100; M. B. Schippers, et al., "Mapping the Information Flow from One Brain to Another During Gestural Communication," *Proceedings of the National Academy of Sciences of the United States of America* 107, no. 20 (2010): 9388–93; and A. N. Meltzoff and J. Decety, "What Imitation Tells Us About Social Cognition: A Rapprochement Between Developmental Psychology and Cognitive Neuroscience," *Philosophical Transactions of the Royal Society, London* 358 (2003): 491–500.
9. D. Goleman, *Emotional Intelligence* (New York: Random House, 2006). See also V. S. Ramachandran, "Mirror Neurons and Imitation Learning as the Driving Force Behind 'the Great Leap Forward' in Human Evolution," Edge (May 31, 2000), http://edge.org/conversation/mirror-neurons-and-imitation-learning-as-the-driving-force-behind-the-great-leap-forward-in-human-evolution (retrieved April 13, 2013).
10. G. M. Edelman, and J. A. Gally, "Reentry: A Key Mechanism for Integration of Brain Function," *Frontiers in Integrative Neuroscience* 7 (2013).
11. J. LeDoux, "Rethinking the Emotional Brain," *Neuron* 73, no. 4 (2012): 653–76. See also J. S. Feinstein, et al., "The Human Amygdala and the Induction and Experience of Fear," *Current Biology* 21, no. 1 (2011): 34–38.
12. The medial prefrontal cortex is the middle part of the brain (neuroscientists call them "the midline structures"). This area of the brain comprises a conglomerate of related structures: the orbito-prefrontal cortex, the inferior and dorsal medial prefrontal cortex, and a large structure called the anterior cingulate, all of which are involved in monitoring the internal state of the organism and selecting the appropriate response. See, e.g., D. Diorio, V. Viau, and M. J. Meaney, "The Role of the Medial Prefrontal Cortex (Cingulate Gyrus) in the Regulation of Hypothalamic-Pituitary-Adrenal Responses to Stress," *Journal of Neuroscience* 13, no. 9 (September 1993): 3839–47; J. P. Mitchell, M. R. Banaji, and C. N. Macrae, "The Link Between Social Cognition and Self-Referential Thought in the Medial Prefrontal Cortex," *Journal of Cognitive Neuroscience* 17, no. 8. (2005): 1306–15; A. D'Argembeau, et al., "Valuing One's Self: Medial Prefrontal Involvement in Epistemic and Emotive Investments in

Self-Views," *Cerebral Cortex* 22 (March 2012): 659–67; M. A. Morgan, L. M. Romanski, J. E. LeDoux, "Extinction of Emotional Learning: Contribution of Medial Prefrontal Cortex," *Neuroscience Letters* 163 (1993):109–13; L. M. Shin, S. L. Rauch, and R. K. Pitman, "Amygdala, Medial Prefrontal Cortex, and Hippocampal Function in PTSD," *Annals of the New York Academy of Sciences* 1071, no. 1 (2006): 67–79; L. M. Williams, et al., "Trauma Modulates Amygdala and Medial Prefrontal Responses to Consciously Attended Fear," Neuroimage, 29, no. 2 (2006): 347–57; M. Koenig and J. Grafman, "Posttraumatic Stress Disorder: The Role of Medial Prefrontal Cortex and Amygdala," *Neuroscientist* 15, no. 5 (2009): 540–48; and M. R. Milad, I. Vidal-Gonzalez, and G. J. Quirk, "Electrical Stimulation of Medial Prefrontal Cortex Reduces Conditioned Fear in a Temporally Specific Manner," *Behavioral Neuroscience* 118, no. 2 (2004): 389.

13. B. A. van der Kolk, "Clinical Implications of Neuroscience Research in PTSD," *Annals of the New York Academy of Sciences* 1071 (2006): 277–93.

14. P. D. MacLean, *The Triune Brain in Evolution: Role in Paleocerebral Functions* (New York, Springer, 1990).

15. Ute Lawrence, *The Power of Trauma: Conquering Post Traumatic Stress Disorder*, iUniverse, 2009.

16. Rita Carter and Christopher D. Frith, *Mapping the Mind* (Berkeley: University of California Press, 1998). See also A. Bechara, et al., "Insensitivity to Future Consequences Following Damage to Human Prefrontal Cortex," *Cognition* 50, no. 1 (1994): 7–15; A. Pascual-Leone, et al., "The Role of the Dorsolateral Prefrontal Cortex in Implicit Procedural Learning," *Experimental Brain Research* 107, no. 3 (1996): 479–85; and S. C. Rao, G. Rainer, and E. K. Miller, "Integration of What and Where in the Primate Prefrontal Cortex," *Science* 276, no. 5313 (1997): 821–24.

17. H. S. Duggal, "New-Onset PTSD After Thalamic Infarct," *American Journal of Psychiatry* 159, no. 12 (2002): 2113-a. See also R. A. Lanius, et al., "Neural Correlates of Traumatic Memories in Posttraumatic Stress Disorder: A Functional MRI Investigation," *American Journal of Psychiatry* 158, no. 11 (2001): 1920–22; and I. Liberzon, et al., "Alteration of Corticothalamic Perfusion Ratios During a PTSD Flashback," *Depression and Anxiety* 4, no. 3 (1996): 146–50.

18. R. Noyes Jr. and R. Kletti, "Depersonalization in Response to Life-Threatening Danger," *Comprehensive Psychiatry* 18, no. 4 (1977): 375–84. See also M. Sierra, and G. E. Berrios, "Depersonalization: Neurobiological Perspectives," *Biological Psychiatry* 44, no. 9 (1998): 898–908.

19. D. Church, et al., "Single-Session Reduction of the Intensity of Traumatic Memories in Abused Adolescents After EFT: A Randomized Controlled Pilot Study," *Traumatology* 18, no. 3 (2012): 73–79; and D. Feinstein and D. Church, "Modulating Gene Expression Through Psychotherapy: The Contribution of Noninvasive Somatic Interventions," *Review of General Psychology* 14, no. 4 (2010): 283–95. See also www.vetcases.com.

CHAPTER 5: BODY-BRAIN CONNECTIONS

1. C. Darwin, *The Expression of the Emotions in Man and Animals* (London: Oxford University Press, 1998).
2. Ibid., 71.
3. Ibid.
4. Ibid., 71–72.
5. P. Ekman, *Facial Action Coding System: A Technique for the Measurement of Facial Movement* (Palo Alto, CA: Consulting Psychologists Press, 1978). See also C. E. Izard, *The Maximally Discriminative Facial Movement Coding System (MAX)* (Newark, DE: University of Delaware Instructional Resource Center, 1979).
6. S. W. Porges, *The Polyvagal Theory: Neurophysiological Foundations of Emotions, Attachment, Communication, and Self-Regulation*, Norton Series on Interpersonal Neurobiology (New York: WW Norton & Company, 2011).
7. This is Stephen Porges's and Sue Carter's name for the ventral vagal system. http://www.pesi.com/bookstore/A_Neural_Love_Code__The_Body_s_Need_to_Engage_and_Bond-details.aspx
8. S. S. Tomkins, *Affect, Imagery, Consciousness* (vol. 1, *The Positive Affects*) (New York: Springer, 1962); S. S. Tomkin, *Affect, Imagery, Consciousness* (vol. 2, *The Negative Affects*) (New York: Springer, 1963).
9. P. Ekman, *Emotions Revealed: Recognizing Faces and Feelings to Improve Communication and Emotional Life* (New York: Macmillan, 2007); P. Ekman, *The Face of Man: Expressions of Universal Emotions in a New Guinea Village* (New York: Garland STPM Press, 1980).
10. See, e.g., B. M. Levinson, "Human/Companion Animal Therapy," *Journal of Contemporary Psychotherapy* 14, no. 2 (1984): 131–44; D. A. Willis, "Animal Therapy," *Rehabilitation Nursing* 22, no. 2 (1997): 78–81; and A. H. Fine, ed., *Handbook on Animal-Assisted Therapy: Theoretical Foundations and Guidelines for Practice* (Academic Press, 2010).
11. P. Ekman, R. W. Levenson, and W. V. Friesen, "Autonomic Nervous System Activity Distinguishes Between Emotions," *Science* 221 (1983): 1208–10.
12. J. H. Jackson, "Evolution and Dissolution of the Nervous System," in *Selected Writings of John Hughlings Jackson*, ed. J. Taylor (London: Stapes Press, 1958), 45–118.
13. Porges pointed out this pet store analogy to me.
14. S. W. Porges, J. A. Doussard-Roosevelt, and A. K. Maiti, "Vagal Tone and the Physiological Regulation of Emotion," in *The Development of Emotion Regulation: Biological and Behavioral Considerations*, ed. N. A. Fox, Monographs of the Society for Research in Child Development, vol. 59 (2–3, serial no. 240) (1994), 167–86. http://www.amazon.com/The-Development-Emotion-Regulation-Considerations/dp/0226259404).
15. V. Felitti, et al., "Relationship of Childhood Abuse and Household Dysfunction to Many of the Leading Causes of Death in Adults: The Adverse Childhood Experiences (ACE) Study," *American Journal of Preventive Medicine* 14, no. 4 (1998): 245–58.
16. S. W. Porges, "Orienting in a Defensive World: Mammalian Modifications of Our Evolutionary Heritage: A Polyvagal Theory," *Psychophysiology* 32 (1995): 301–18.
17. B. A. Van der Kolk, "The Body Keeps the Score: Memory and the Evolving Psychobiology of Posttraumatic Stress," *Harvard Review of Psychiatry* 1, no. 5 (1994): 253–65.

CHAPTER 6: LOSING YOUR BODY, LOSING YOUR SELF

1. K. L. Walsh, et al., "Resiliency Factors in the Relation Between Childhood Sexual Abuse and Adulthood Sexual Assault in College-Age Women," *Journal of Child Sexual Abuse* 16, no. 1 (2007): 1–17.

2. A. C. McFarlane, "The Long-Term Costs of Traumatic Stress: Intertwined Physical and Psychological Consequences," *World Psychiatry* 9, no. 1 (2010): 3–10.

3. W. James, "What Is an Emotion?" *Mind* 9: 188–205.

4. R. L. Bluhm, et al., "Alterations in Default Network Connectivity in Posttraumatic Stress Disorder Related to Early-Life Trauma," *Journal of Psychiatry & Neuroscience* 34, no. 3 (2009): 187. See also J. K. Daniels, et al., "Switching Between Executive and Default Mode Networks in Posttraumatic Stress Disorder: Alterations in Functional Connectivity," *Journal of Psychiatry & Neuroscience* 35, no. 4 (2010): 258.

5. A. Damasio, *The Feeling of What Happens: Body and Emotion in the Making of Consciousness* (New York: Hartcourt Brace, 1999). Damasio actually says, "Consciousness was invented so that we could know life", p. 31.

6. Damasio, *Feeling of What Happens*, p. 28.

7. Ibid., p. 29.

8. A. Damasio, *Self Comes to Mind: Constructing the Conscious Brain* (New York, Random House Digital, 2012), 17.

9. Damasio, *Feeling of What Happens*, p. 256.

10. Antonio R. Damasio, et al., "Subcortical and Cortical Brain Activity During the Feeling of Self-Generated Emotions." *Nature Neuroscience* 3, vol. 10 (2000): 1049–56.

11. A. A. T. S. Reinders, et al., "One Brain, Two Selves," *NeuroImage* 20 (2003): 2119–25. See also E. R. S. Nijenhuis, O. Van der Hart, and K. Steele, "The Emerging Psychobiology of Trauma-Related Dissociation and Dissociative Disorders," in *Biological Psychiatry*, vol. 2., eds. H. A. H. D'Haenen, J. A. den Boer, and P. Willner (West Sussex, UK: Wiley 2002), 1079–198; J. Parvizi and A. R. Damasio, "Consciousness and the Brain Stem," *Cognition* 79 (2001): 135–59; F. W. Putnam, "Dissociation and Disturbances of Self," in *Dysfunctions of the Self*, vol. 5, eds. D. Cicchetti and S. L. Toth (New York: University of Rochester Press, 1994), 251–65; and F. W. Putnam, *Dissociation in Children and Adolescents: A Developmental Perspective* (New York: Guilford, 1997).

12. A. D'Argembeau, et al., "Distinct Regions of the Medial Prefrontal Cortex Are Associated with Self-Referential Processing and Perspective Taking," *Journal of Cognitive Neuroscience* 19, no. 6 (2007): 935–44. See also N. A. Farb, et al., "Attending to the Present: Mindfulness Meditation Reveals Distinct Neural Modes of Self-Reference," *Social Cognitive and Affective Neuroscience* 2, no. 4 (2007): 313–22; and B. K. Hölzel, et al., "Investigation of Mindfulness Meditation Practitioners with Voxel-Based Morphometry," *Social Cognitive and Affective Neuroscience* 3, no. 1 (2008): 55–61.

13. P. A. Levine, *Healing Trauma: A Pioneering Program for Restoring the Wisdom of Your Body* (Berkeley: North Atlantic Books, 2008); and P. A. Levine, *In an Unspoken Voice: How the Body Releases Trauma and Restores Goodness* (Berkeley: North Atlantic Books, 2010).

14. P. Ogden and K. Minton, "Sensorimotor Psychotherapy: One Method for Processing Traumatic Memory," *Traumatology* 6, no. 3 (2000): 149–73; and P. Ogden, K. Minton, and C. Pain, *Trauma and the Body: A Sensorimotor Approach to Psychotherapy*, Norton Series on Interpersonal Neurobiology (New York: WW Norton & Company, 2006).

15. D. A. Bakal, *Minding the Body: Clinical Uses of Somatic Awareness* (New York: Guilford Press, 2001).

16. There are innumerable studies on the subject. A small sample for further study: J. Wolfe, et al., "Posttraumatic Stress Disorder and War-Zone Exposure as Correlates of Perceived Health in Female Vietnam War Veterans," *Journal of Consulting and Clinical Psychology* 62, no. 6 (1994): 1235–40; L. A. Zoellner, M. L. Goodwin, and E. B. Foa, "PTSD Severity and Health Perceptions in Female Victims

of Sexual Assault," *Journal of Traumatic Stress* 13, no. 4 (2000): 635–49; E. M. Sledjeski, B. Speisman, and L. C. Dierker, "Does Number of Lifetime Traumas Explain the Relationship Between PTSD and Chronic Medical Conditions? Answers from the National Comorbidity Survey-Replication (NCS-R)," *Journal of Behavioral Medicine* 31 (2008): 341–49; J. A. Boscarino, "Posttraumatic Stress Disorder and Physical Illness: Results from Clinical and Epidemiologic Studies," *Annals of the New York Academy of Sciences* 1032 (2004): 141–53; M. Cloitre, et al., "Posttraumatic Stress Disorder and Extent of Trauma Exposure as Correlates of Medical Problems and Perceived Health Among Women with Childhood Abuse," *Women & Health* 34, no. 3 (2001): 1–17; D. Lauterbach, R. Vora, and M. Rakow, "The Relationship Between Posttraumatic Stress Disorder and Self-Reported Health Problems," *Psychosomatic Medicine* 67, no. 6 (2005): 939–47; B. S. McEwen, "Protective and Damaging Effects of Stress Mediators," *New England Journal of Medicine* 338, no. 3 (1998): 171–79; P. P. Schnurr and B. L. Green, *Trauma and Health: Physical Health Consequences of Exposure to Extreme Stress* (Washington, DC: American Psychological Association, 2004).

17. P. K. Trickett, J. G. Noll, and F. W. Putnam, "The Impact of Sexual Abuse on Female Development: Lessons from a Multigenerational, Longitudinal Research Study," *Development and Psychopathology* 23, no. 2 (2011): 453.

18. K. Kosten and F. Giller Jr., "Alexithymia as a Predictor of Treatment Response in PostTraumatic Stress Disorder," *Journal of Traumatic Stress* 5, no. 4 (October 1992): 563–73.

19. G. J. Taylor and R. M. Bagby, "New Trends in Alexithymia Research," *Psychotherapy and Psychosomatics* 73, no. 2 (2004): 68–77.

20. R. D. Lane, et al., "Impaired Verbal and Nonverbal Emotion Recognition in Alexithymia," *Psychosomatic Medicine* 58, no. 3 (1996): 203–10.

21. H. Krystal and J. H. Krystal, *Integration and Self-Healing: Affect, Trauma, Alexithymia* (New York: Analytic Press, 1988).

22. P. Frewen, et al., "Clinical and Neural Correlates of Alexithymia in Posttraumatic Stress Disorder," *Journal of Abnormal Psychology* 117, no. 1 (2008): 171–81.

23. D. Finkelhor, R. K. Ormrod, and H. A. Turner, (2007). "Re-Victimization Patterns in a National Longitudinal Sample of Children and Youth," *Child Abuse & Neglect* 31, no. 5 (2007): 479-502; J. A. Schumm, S. E. Hobfoll, and N. J. Keogh, "Revictimization and Interpersonal Resource Loss Predicts PTSD Among Women in Substance-Use Treatment, *Journal of Traumatic Stress,* 17, no. 2 (2004): 173–81; J. D. Ford, J. D. Elhai, D. F. Connor, and B. C. Frueh, "Poly-Victimization and Risk of Posttraumatic, Depressive, and Substance Use Disorders and Involvement in Delinquency in a National Sample of Adolescents," *Journal of Adolescent Health,* 46, no. 6 (2010): 545–52.

24. P. Schilder, "Depersonalization," in *Introduction to a Psychoanalytic Psychiatry,* no. 50 (New York: International Universities Press, 196), p. 120.

25. S. Arzy, et al., "Neural Mechanisms of Embodiment: Asomatognosia Due to Premotor Cortex Damage," *Archives of Neurology* 63, no. 7 (2006): 1022–25. See also S. Arzy et al., "Induction of an Illusory Shadow Person," *Nature* 443, no. 7109 (2006): 287; S. Arzy et al., "Neural Basis of Embodiment: Distinct Contributions of Temporoparietal Junction and Extrastriate Body Area," *Journal of Neuroscience* 26, no. 31 (2006): 8074–81; O. Blanke et al., "Out-of-Body Experience and Autoscopy of Neurological Origin," *Brain* 127, part 2 (2004): 243–58; and M. Sierra, et al., "Unpacking the Depersonalization Syndrome: An Exploratory Factor Analysis on the Cambridge Depersonalization Scale," *Psychological Medicine* 35 (2005): 1523–32.

26. A. A. T. Reinders, et al., "Psychobiological Characteristics of Dissociative Identity Disorder: A Symptom Provocation Study," *Biological Psychiatry* 60, no. 7 (2006): 730–40.

27. In his book *Focusing,* Eugene Gendlin coined the term "felt sense": "A felt sense is not a mental experience but a physical one. A bodily awareness of a situation or person or event; *Focusing* (New York, Random House Digital, 1982).

28. C. Steuwe, et al., "Effect of Direct Eye Contact in PTSD Related to Interpersonal Trauma: An fMRI Study of Activation of an Innate Alarm System," *Social Cognitive and Affective Neuroscience* 9, no. 1

(January 2012): 88–97.

CHAPTER 7: GETTING ON THE SAME WAVELENGTH, ATTACHMENT AND ATTUNEMENT

1. N. Murray, E. Koby, and B. van der Kolk, "The Effects of Abuse on Children's Thoughts," chapter 4 in *Psychological Trauma* (Washington, DC: American Psychiatric Press, 1987).

2. The attachment researcher Mary Main told six-year-olds a story about a child whose mother had gone away and asked them to make up a story of what happened next. Most six-year-olds who, as infants, had been found to have secure relationships with their mothers made up some imaginative tale with a good ending, while the kids who five years earlier had been classified as having a disorganized attachment relationship had a tendency toward catastrophic fantasies and often gave frightened responses like "The parents will die" or "The child will kill herself." In Mary Main, Nancy Kaplan, and Jude Cassidy. "Security in Infancy, Childhood, and Adulthood: A Move to the Level of Representation," *Monographs of the Society for Research in Child Development* (1985).

3. J. Bowlby, *Attachment and Loss*, vol. 1, *Attachment* (New York Random House, 1969); J. Bowlby, *Attachment and Loss*, vol. 2, *Separation: Anxiety and Anger* (New York: Penguin, 1975); J. Bowlby, *Attachment and Loss*, vol. 3, *Loss: Sadness and Depression* (New York: Basic, 1980); J. Bowlby, "The Nature of the Child's Tie to His Mother 1," *International Journal of Psycho-Analysis*, 1958, 39, 350–73.

4. C. Trevarthen, "Musicality and the Intrinsic Motive Pulse: Evidence from Human Psychobiology and Rhythms, Musical Narrative, and the Origins of Human Communication," *Muisae Scientiae*, special issue, 1999, 157–213.

5. A. Gopnik and A. N. Meltzoff, *Words, Thoughts, and Theories* (Cambridge: MIT Press, 1997); A. N. Meltzoff and M. K. Moore, "Newborn Infants Imitate Adult Facial Gestures," *Child Development* 54, no. 3 (June 1983): 702–9; A. Gopnik, A. N. Meltzoff, and P. K. Kuhl, *The Scientist in the Crib: Minds, Brains, and How Children Learn* (New York: HarperCollins, 2009).

6. E. Z. Tronick, "Emotions and Emotional Communication in Infants," *American Psychologist* 44, no. 2 (1989): 112. See also E. Tronick, *The Neurobehavioral and Social-Emotional Development of Infants and Children* (New York, WW Norton & Company, 2007); E. Tronick and M. Beeghly, "Infants' Meaning-Making and the Development of Mental Health Problems," *American Psychologist* 66, no. 2 (2011): 107; and A. V. Sravish, et al., "Dyadic Flexibility During the Face-to-Face Still-Face Paradigm: A Dynamic Systems Analysis of Its Temporal Organization," *Infant Behavior and Development* 36, no. 3 (2013): 432–37.

7. M. Main, "Overview of the Field of Attachment," *Journal of Consulting and Clinical Psychology* 64, no. 2 (1996): 237–43.

8. D. W. Winnicott, *Playing and Reality* (New York: Psychology Press, 1971). See also D. W. Winnicott, "The Maturational Processes and the Facilitating Environment," (1965); and D. W. Winnicott, *Through Paediatrics to Psychoanalysis: Collected Papers* (New York: Brunner/Mazel, 1975).

9. As we saw in chapter 6, and as Damasio has demonstrated, this sense of inner reality is, at least in part, rooted in the insula, the brain structure that plays a central role in body-mind communication, a structure that is often impaired in people with histories of chronic trauma.

10. D. W. Winnicott, *Primary Maternal Preoccupation* (London: Tavistock, 1956), 300–305.

11. S. D. Pollak, et al., "Recognizing Emotion in Faces: Developmental Effects of Child Abuse and Neglect," *Developmental Psychology* 36, no. 5 (2000): 679.

12. P. M. Crittenden, "IV Peering into the Black Box: An Exploratory Treatise on the Development of Self in Young Children," *Disorders and Dysfunctions of the Self* 5 (1994): 79; P. M. Crittenden, and A. Landini, *Assessing Adult Attachment: A Dynamic-Maturational Approach to Discourse Analysis* (New York: WW Norton & Company, 2011).

13. Patricia M. Crittenden, "Children's Strategies for Coping with Adverse Home Environments: An Interpretation Using Attachment Theory," *Child Abuse & Neglect* 16, no. 3 (1992): 329–43.

14. Main, 1990, op cit.

15. Main, 1990, op cit.

16. Ibid.

17. E. Hesse, and M. Main, "Frightened, Threatening, and Dissociative Parental Behavior in Low-Risk Samples: Description, Discussion, and Interpretations," *Development and Psychopathology* 18, no. 2 (2006): 309–343. See also E. Hesse and M. Main, "Disorganized Infant, Child, and Adult Attachment: Collapse in Behavioral and Attentional Strategies," *Journal of the American Psychoanalytic Association* 48, no. 4 (2000): 1097–127.

18. Main, "Overview of the Field of Attachment," op cit.

19. Hesse and Main, 1995, op cit, p. 310.

20. We looked at this from a biological point of view when we discussed "immobilization without fear" in chapter 5. S. W. Porges, "Orienting in a Defensive World: Mammalian Modifications of Our Evolutionary Heritage: A Polyvagal Theory," *Psychophysiology* 32 (1995): 301–318.

21. M. H. van Ijzendoorn, C. Schuengel, and M. Bakermans-Kranenburg, "Disorganized Attachment in Early Childhood: Meta-analysis of Precursors, Concomitants, and Sequelae," *Development and Psychopathology* 11 (1999): 225–49.

22. Ijzendoorn, op cit.

23. N. W. Boris, M. Fueyo, and C. H. Zeanah, "The Clinical Assessment of Attachment in Children Under Five," *Journal of the American Academy of Child & Adolescent Psychiatry,* 36, no. 2 (1997): 291–93; K. Lyons-Ruth, "Attachment Relationships Among Children with Aggressive Behavior Problems: The Role of Disorganized Early Attachment Patterns," *Journal of Consulting and Clinical Psychology,* 64, no. 1 (1996), 64.

24. Stephen W. Porges, et al., "Infant Regulation of the Vagal 'Brake' Predicts Child Behavior Problems: A Psychobiological Model of Social Behavior," *Developmental Psychobiology* 29, no. 8 (1996): 697–712.

25. Louise Hertsgaard, et al., "Adrenocortical Responses to the Strange Situation in Infants with Disorganized/Disoriented Attachment Relationships," *Child Development* 66, no. 4 (1995): 1100–6; Gottfried Spangler, and Klaus E. Grossmann, "Biobehavioral Organization in Securely and Insecurely Attached Infants," *Child Development* 64, no. 5 (1993): 1439–50.

26. Main and Hesse, 1990, op cit.

27. M. H. van Ijzendoorn, et al., "Disorganized Attachment in Early Childhood," op cit.

28. B. Beebe, and F. M. Lachmann, *Infant Research and Adult Treatment: Co-constructing Interactions* (New York: Routledge, 2013); B. Beebe, F. Lachmann, and J. Jaffe (1997). Mother-Infant Interaction Structures and Presymbolic Self-and Object Representations. *Psychoanalytic Dialogues,* 7, no. 2 (1997): 133–82.

29. R. Yehuda, et al., "Vulnerability to Posttraumatic Stress Disorder in Adult Offspring of Holocaust Survivors," *American Journal of Psychiatry* 155, no. 9 (1998): 1163–71. See also R. Yehuda, et al., "Relationship Between Posttraumatic Stress Disorder Characteristics of Holocaust Survivors and Their Adult Offspring," *American Journal of Psychiatry* 155, no. 6 (1998): 841–43; R. Yehuda, et al., "Parental Posttraumatic Stress Disorder as a Vulnerability Factor for Low Cortisol Trait in Offspring of Holocaust Survivors," *Archives of General Psychiatry* 64, no. 9 (2007): 1040 and R. Yehuda, et al., "Maternal, Not Paternal, PTSD Is Related to Increased Risk for PTSD in Offspring of Holocaust Survivors," *Journal of Psychiatric Research* 42, no. 13 (2008): 1104–11.

30. R. Yehuda, et al., "Transgenerational Effects of PTSD in Babies of Mothers Exposed to the WTC Attacks During Pregnancy," *Journal of Clinical Endocrinology and Metabolism* 90 (2005): 4115–18.

31. G. Saxe, et al., "Relationship Between Acute Morphine and the Course of PTSD in Children with Burns," *Journal of the American Academy of Child & Adolescent Psychiatry* 40, no. 8 (2001): 915–21. See also G. N. Saxe, et al., "Pathways to PTSD, Part I: Children with Burns," *American Journal of Psychiatry* 162, no. 7 (2005): 1299–304.

32. C. M. Chemtob, Y. Nomura, and R. A. Abramovitz, "Impact of Conjoined Exposure to the World

Trade Center Attacks and to Other Traumatic Events on the Behavioral Problems of Preschool Children," *Archives of Pediatrics and Adolescent Medicine* 162, no. 2 (2008): 126. See also P. J. Landrigan, et al., "Impact of September 11 World Trade Center Disaster on Children and Pregnant Women," *Mount Sinai Journal of Medicine* 75, no. 2 (2008): 129–34.

33. D. Finkelhor, R. K. Ormrod, and H. A. Turner, "Polyvictimization and Trauma in a National Longitudinal Cohort," *Development and Psychopathology* 19, no. 1 (2007): 149–66; J. D. Ford, et al., "Polyvictimization and Risk of Posttraumatic, Depressive, and Substance Use Disorders and Involvement in Delinquency in a National Sample of Adolescents," *Journal of Adolescent Health* 46, no. 6 (2010): 545–52; J. D. Ford, et al., "Clinical Significance of a Proposed Development Trauma Disorder Diagnosis: Results of an International Survey of Clinicians," *Journal of Clinical Psychiatry* 74, no. 8 (2013): 841–49.

34. Family Pathways Project, http://www.challiance.org/academics/familypathwaysproject.aspx.

35. K. Lyons-Ruth and D. Block, "The Disturbed Caregiving System: Relations Among Childhood Trauma, Maternal Caregiving, and Infant Affect and Attachment," *Infant Mental Health Journal* 17, no. 3 (1996): 257–75.

36. K. Lyons-Ruth, "The Two-Person Construction of Defenses: Disorganized Attachment Strategies, Unintegrated Mental States, and Hostile/Helpless Relational Processes," *Journal of Infant, Child, and Adolescent Psychotherapy* 2 (2003): 105.

37. G. Whitmer, "On the Nature of Dissociation," *Psychoanalytic Quarterly* 70, no. 4 (2001): 807–37. See also K. Lyons-Ruth, "The Two-Person Construction of Defenses: Disorganized Attachment Strategies, Unintegrated Mental States, and Hostile/Helpless Relational Processes," *Journal of Infant, Child, and Adolescent Psychotherapy* 2, no. 4 (2002): 107–19.

38. Mary S. Ainsworth and John Bowlby, "An Ethological Approach to Personality Development," *American Psychologist* 46, no. 4 (April 1991): 333–41.

39. K. Lyons-Ruth and D. Jacobvitz, 1999; Main, 1993; K. Lyons-Ruth, "Dissociation and the Parent-Infant Dialogue: A Longitudinal Perspective from Attachment Research," *Journal of the American Psychoanalytic Association* 51, no. 3 (2003): 883–911.

40. L. Dutra, et al., "Quality of Early Care and Childhood Trauma: A Prospective Study of Developmental Pathways to Dissociation," *Journal of Nervous and Mental Disease* 197, no. 6 (2009): 383. See also K. Lyons-Ruth, et al., "Borderline Symptoms and Suicidality/Self-Injury in Late Adolescence: Prospectively Observed Relationship Correlates in Infancy and Childhood," *Psychiatry Research* 206, nos. 2–3 (April 30, 2013): 273–81.

41. For meta-analysis of the relative contributions of disorganized attachment and child maltreatment, see C. Schuengel, et al., "Frightening Maternal Behavior Linking Unresolved Loss and Disorganized Infant Attachment," *Journal of Consulting and Clinical Psychology* 67, no. 1 (1999): 54.

42. K. Lyons-Ruth and D. Jacobvitz, "Attachment Disorganization: Genetic Factors, Parenting Contexts, and Developmental Transformation from Infancy to Adulthood," in *Handbook of Attachment: Theory, Research, and Clinical Applications*, 2nd ed., ed. J. Cassidy and R. Shaver (New York: Guilford Press, 2008), 666–97. See also E. O'connor, et al., "Risks and Outcomes Associated with Disorganized/Controlling Patterns of Attachment at Age Three Years in the National Institute of Child Health & Human Development Study of Early Child Care and Youth Development," *Infant Mental Health Journal 32*, no. 4 (2011): 450–72; and K. Lyons-Ruth, et al., "Borderline Symptoms and Suicidality/Self-Injury.

43. At this point we have little information about what factors affect the evolution of these early regulatory abnormalities, but intervening life events, the quality of other relationships, and perhaps even genetic factors are likely to modify them over time. It is obviously critical to study to what degree consistent and concentrated parenting of children with early histories of abuse and neglect can rearrange biological systems.

44. E. Warner, et al., "Can the Body Change the Score? Application of Sensory Modulation Principles in the Treatment of Traumatized Adolescents in Residential Settings," *Journal of Family Violence* 28, no.

7 (2003): 729–38.

CHAPTER 8: TRAPPED IN RELATIONSHIPS: THE COST OF ABUSE AND NEGLECT

1. W. H. Auden, *The Double Man* (New York: Random House, 1941),
2. S. N. Wilson, et al., "Phenotype of Blood Lymphocytes in PTSD Suggests Chronic Immune Activation," *Psychosomatics* 40, no. 3 (1999): 222–25. See also M. Uddin, et al., "Epigenetic and Immune Function Profiles Associated with Posttraumatic Stress Disorder," *Proceedings of the National Academy of Sciences of the United States of America* 107, no. 20 (2010): 9470–75; M. Altemus, M. Cloitre, and F. S. Dhabhar, "Enhanced Cellular Immune Response in Women with PTSD Related to Childhood Abuse," *American Journal of Psychiatry* 160, no. 9 (2003): 1705–7; and N. Kawamura, Y. Kim, and N. Asukai, "Suppression of Cellular Immunity in Men with a Past History of Posttraumatic Stress Disorder," *American Journal of Psychiatry* 158, no. 3 (2001): 484–86.
3. R. Summit, "The Child Sexual Abuse Accommodation Syndrome," *Child Abuse & Neglect* 7 (1983): 177–93.
4. A study using fMRI at the University of Lausanne in Switzerland showed that when people have these out-of-body experiences, staring at themselves as if looking down from the ceiling, they are activating the superior temporal cortex in the brain. O. Blanke, et al., "Linking Out-of-Body Experience and Self Processing to Mental Own-Body Imagery at the Temporoparietal Junction," *Journal of Neuroscience* 25, no. 3 (2005): 550–57. See also O. Blanke and T. Metzinger, "Full-Body Illusions and Minimal Phenomenal Selfhood," *Trends in Cognitive Sciences* 13, no. 1 (2009): 7–13.
5. When an adult uses a child for sexual gratification, the child invariably is caught in a confusing situation and a conflict of loyalties: By disclosing the abuse, she betrays and hurts the perpetrator (who may be an adult on whom the child depends for safety and protection), but by hiding the abuse, she compounds her shame and vulnerability. This dilemma was first articulated by Sándor Ferenczi in 1933 in "The Confusion of Tongues Between the Adult and the Child: The Language of Tenderness and the Language of Passion," *International Journal of Psychoanalysis*, 30 no. 4 (1949): 225–30, and has been explored by numerous subsequent authors.

CHAPTER 9: WHAT'S LOVE GOT TO DO WITH IT?

1. Gary Greenberg, The Book of Woe: The DSM and the Unmaking of Psychiatry (New York: Penguin, 2013).
2. http://www.thefreedictionary.com/diagnosis.
3. The TAQ can be accessed at the Trauma Center Web site: www.traumacenter.org/products/instruments.php.
4. J. L. Herman, J. C. Perry, and B. A. van der Kolk, "Childhood Trauma in Borderline Personality Disorder," *American Journal of Psychiatry* 146, no. 4 (April 1989): 490–95.
5. Teicher found significant changes in the orbitofrontal cortex (OFC), a region of the brain that is involved in decision making and the regulation of behavior involved in sensitivity to social demands. M. H. Teicher, et al., "The Neurobiological Consequences of Early Stress and Childhood Maltreatment," *Neuroscience & Biobehavioral Reviews* 27, no. 1 (2003): 33–44. See also M. H. Teicher, "Scars That Won't Heal: The Neurobiology of Child Abuse," *Scientific American* 286, no. 3 (2002): 54–61; M. Teicher, et al., "Sticks, Stones, and Hurtful Words: Relative Effects of Various Forms of Childhood Maltreatment," *American Journal of Psychiatry* 163, no. 6 (2006): 993–1000; A. Bechara, et al., "Insensitivity to Future Consequences Following Damage to Human Prefrontal Cortex," *Cognition* 50 (1994): 7–15. Impairment in this area of the brain results in excessive swearing, poor social interactions, compulsive gambling, excessive alcohol / drug use and poor empathic ability. M. L. Kringelbach and E. T. Rolls, "The Functional Neuroanatomy of the Human Orbitofrontal Cortex: Evidence from Neuroimaging and Neuropsychology," *Progress in Neurobiology* 72 (2004):

341–72. The other problematic area Teicher identified was the precuneus, a brain area involved in understanding oneself and being able to take perspective on how your perceptions may be different from someone else's. A. E. Cavanna and M. R. Trimble "The Precuneus: A Review of Its Functional Anatomy and Behavioural Correlates," *Brain* 129 (2006): 564–83.

6. S. Roth, et al., "Complex PTSD in Victims Exposed to Sexual and Physical Abuse: Results from the DSM-IV Field Trial for Posttraumatic Stress Disorder," *Journal of Traumatic Stress* 10 (1997): 539–55; B. A. van der Kolk et al., "Dissociation, Somatization, and Affect Dysregulation: The Complexity of Adaptation to Trauma," *American Journal of Psychiatry* 153 (1996): 83–93; D. Pelcovitz, et al., "Development of a Criteria Set and a Structured Interview for Disorders of Extreme Stress (SIDES)," *Journal of Traumatic Stress* 10 (1997): 3–16; S. N. Ogata, et al., "Childhood Sexual and Physical Abuse in Adult Patients with Borderline Personality Disorder," *American Journal of Psychiatry* 147 (1990): 1008–1013; M. C. Zanarini, et al., "Axis I Comorbidity of Borderline Personality Disorder," *American Journal of Psychiatry* 155, no. 12. (December 1998): 1733–39; S. L. Shearer, et al., "Frequency and Correlates of Childhood Sexual and Physical Abuse Histories in Adult Female Borderline Inpatients," *American Journal of Psychiatry* 147 (1990): 214–16; D. Westen, et al., "Physical and Sexual Abuse in Adolescent Girls with Borderline Personality Disorder," *American Journal of Orthopsychiatry* 60 (1990): 55–66; M. C. Zanarini, et al., "Reported Pathological Childhood Experiences Associated with the Development of Borderline Personality Disorder," American Journal of Psychiatry 154 (1997): 1101–1106.

7. J. Bowlby, *A Secure Base: Parent-Child Attachment and Healthy Human Development* (New York: Basic Books, 2008), 103.

8. B. A. van der Kolk, J. C. Perry, and J. L. Herman, "Childhood Origins of Self-Destructive Behavior," *American Journal of Psychiatry* 148 (1991): 1665–71.

9. This notion found further support in the work of the neuroscientist Jaak Panksepp, who found that young rats that were not licked by their moms during the first week of their lives did not develop opioid receptors in the anterior cingulate cortex, a part of the brain associated with affiliation and a sense of safety. See E. E. Nelson and J. Panksepp, "Brain Substrates of Infant-Mother Attachment: Contributions of Opioids, Oxytocin, and Norepinephrine," *Neuroscience & Biobehavioral Reviews* 22, no. 3 (1998): 437–52. See also J. Panksepp, et al., "Endogenous Opioids and Social Behavior," *Neuroscience & Biobehavioral Reviews* 4, no. 4 (1981): 473–87; and J. Panksepp, E. Nelson, and S. Siviy, "Brain Opioids and Mother-Infant Social Motivation," *Acta paediatrica* 83, no. 397 (1994): 40–46.

10. The delegation to Robert Spitzer also included Judy Herman, Jim Chu, and David Pelcovitz.

11. B. A. van der Kolk, et al., "Disorders of Extreme Stress: The Empirical Foundation of a Complex Adaptation to Trauma," *Journal of Traumatic Stress* 18, no. 5 (2005): 389–99. See also J. L. Herman, "Complex PTSD: A Syndrome in Survivors of Prolonged and Repeated Trauma," *Journal of Traumatic Stress* 5, no. 3 (1992): 377–91; C. Zlotnick, et al., "The Long-Term Sequelae of Sexual Abuse: Support for a Complex Posttraumatic Stress Disorder," *Journal of Traumatic Stress* 9, no. 2 (1996): 195–205; S. Roth, et al., "Complex PTSD in Victims Exposed to Sexual and Physical Abuse: Results from the DSM-IV Field Trial for Posttraumatic Stress Disorder," *Journal of Traumatic Stress* 10, no. 4 (1997): 539–55; and D. Pelcovitz, et al., "Development and Validation of the Structured Interview for Measurement of Disorders of Extreme Stress," *Journal of Traumatic Stress* 10 *(1997)*: 3–16.

12. B. C. Stolbach, et al., "Complex Trauma Exposure and Symptoms in Urban Traumatized Children: A Preliminary Test of Proposed Criteria for Developmental Trauma Disorder," *Journal of Traumatic Stress* 26, no. 4 (August 2013): 483–91.

13. B. A. van der Kolk, et al., "Dissociation, Somatization and Affect Dysregulation: The Complexity of Adaptation to Trauma," *American Journal of Psychiatry* 153, suppl (1996): 83–93. See also D. G. Kilpatrick, et al., "Posttraumatic Stress Disorder Field Trial: Evaluation of the PTSD Construct—Criteria A Through E," in: *DSM-IV Sourcebook*, vol. 4 (Washington: American Psychiatric Press,

1998), 803-844; T. Luxenberg, J. Spinazzola, and B. A. van der Kolk, "Complex Trauma and Disorders of Extreme Stress (DESNOS) Diagnosis, Part One: Assessment," *Directions in Psychiatry* 21, no. 25 (2001): 373–92; and B. A. van der Kolk, et al., "Disorders of Extreme Stress: The Empirical Foundation of a Compex Adaptation to Trauma," *Journal of Traumatic Stress* 18, no. 5 (2005): 389–99.

14. These questions are available on the ACE Web site: http://acestudy.org/.

15. http://www.cdc.gov/ace/findings.htm; http://acestudy.org/download; V. Felitti, et al., "Relationship of Childhood Abuse and Household Dysfunction to Many of the Leading Causes of Death in Adults: The Adverse Childhood Experiences (ACE) Study," *American Journal of Preventive Medicine* 14, no. 4 (1998): 245–58. See also R. Reading, "The Enduring Effects of Abuse and Related Adverse Experiences in Childhood: A Convergence of Evidence from Neurobiology and Epidemiology," *Child: Care, Health and Development* 32, no. 2 (2006): 253–56; V. J. Edwards, et al., "Experiencing Multiple Forms of Childhood Maltreatment and Adult Mental Health: Results from the Adverse Childhood Experiences (ACE) Study," *American Journal of Psychiatry* 160, no. 8 (2003): 1453–60; S. R. Dube, et al., "Adverse Childhood Experiences and Personal Alcohol Abuse as an Adult," *Addictive Behaviors* 27, no. 5 (2002): 713–25; S. R. and S. R. Dube, et al., "Childhood Abuse, Neglect, and Household Dysfunction and the Risk of Illicit Drug Use: The Adverse Childhood Experiences Study," *Pediatrics* 111, no. 3 (2003): 564–72.

16. S. A. Strassels, "Economic Burden of Prescription Opioid Misuse and Abuse," *Journal of Managed Care Pharmacy* 15, no. 7 (2009): 556–62.

17. C. B. Nemeroff, et al., "Differential Responses to Psychotherapy Versus Pharmacotherapy in Patients with Chronic Forms of Major Depression and Childhood Trauma," *Proceedings of the National Academy of Sciences of the United States of America* 100, no. 24 (2003): 14293–96. See also C. Heim, P. M. Plotsky, and C. B. Nemeroff, "Importance of Studying the Contributions of Early Adverse Experience to Neurobiological Findings in Depression," *Neuropsychopharmacology* 29, no. 4 (2004): 641–48.

18. B. E. Carlson, "Adolescent Observers of Marital Violence," *Journal of Family Violence* 5, no. 4 (1990): 285–99. See also B. E. Carlson, "Children's Observations of Interparental Violence," in *Battered Women and Their Families*, ed. A. R. Roberts (New York: Springer, 1984), 147–67; J. L. Edleson, "Children's Witnessing of Adult Domestic Violence," *Journal of Interpersonal Violence* 14, no. 8 (1999): 839–70; K. Henning, et al., "Long-Term Psychological and Social Impact of Witnessing Physical Conflict Between Parents," *Journal of Interpersonal Violence* 11, no. 1 (1996): 35–51; E. N. Jouriles, C. M. Murphy, and D. O'Leary, "Interpersonal Aggression, Marital Discord, and Child Problems," *Journal of Consulting and Clinical Psychology* 57, no. 3 (1989): 453–55; J. R. Kolko, E. H. Blakely, and D. Engelman, "Children Who Witness Domestic Violence: A Review of Empirical Literature," *Journal of Interpersonal Violence* 11, no. 2 (1996): 281–93; and J. Wolak and D. Finkelhor, "Children Exposed to Partner Violence," in *Partner Violence: A Comprehensive Review of 20 Years of Research*, ed. J. L. Jasinski and L. Williams (Thousand Oaks, CA: Sage, 1998).

19. Most of these statements are based on conversations with Vincent Felitti, amplified by J. E. Stevens, "The Adverse Childhood Experiences Study—the Largest Public Health Study You Never Heard Of," *Huffington Post*, October 8, 2012, http://www.huffingtonpost.com/jane-ellen-stevens/the-adverse-childhood-exp 1b_1943647.html.

20. Population attributable risk: the proportion of a problem in the overall population whose problems can be attributed to specific risk factors.

21. National Cancer Institute, "Nearly 800,000 Deaths Prevented Due to Declines in Smoking" (press release), March 14, 2012, available at http://www.cancer.gov/newscenter/newsfromnci/2012/TobaccoControlCISNET.

CHAPTER 10: DEVELOPMENTAL TRAUMA: THE HIDDEN EPIDEMIC

1. These cases were part of the DTD field trial, conducted jointly by Julian Ford, Joseph Spinazzola, and me.

2. H. J. Williams, M. J. Owen, and M. C. O'Donovan, "Schizophrenia Genetics: New Insights from New Approaches," *British Medical Bulletin* 91 (2009): 61–74. See also P. V. Gejman, A. R. Sanders, and K. S. Kendler, "Genetics of Schizophrenia: New Findings and Challenges," *Annual Review of Genomics and Human Genetics* 12 (2011): 121–44; and A. Sanders, et al., "No Significant Association of 14 Candidate Genes with Schizophrenia in a Large European Ancestry Sample: Implications for Psychiatric Genetics," *American Journal of Psychiatry* 165, no. 4 (April 2008): 497–506.

3. R. Yehuda, et al., "Putative Biological Mechanisms for the Association Between Early Life Adversity and the Subsequent Development of PTSD," *Psychopharmacology* 212, no. 3 (October 2010): 405–417; K. C. Koenen, "Genetics of Posttraumatic Stress Disorder: Review and Recommendations for Future Studies," *Journal of Traumatic Stress* 20, no. 5 (October 2007): 737–50; M. W. Gilbertson, et al., "Smaller Hippocampal Volume Predicts Pathologic Vulnerability to Psychological Trauma," *Nature Neuroscience* 5 (2002): 1242–47.

4. Koenen, "Genetics of Posttraumatic Stress Disorder." See also R. F. P. Broekman, M. Olff, and F. Boer, "The Genetic Background to PTSD," *Neuroscience & Biobehavioral Reviews* 31, no. 3 (2007): 348–62.

5. M. J. Meaney and A. C. Ferguson-Smith, "Epigenetic Regulation of the Neural Transcriptome: The Meaning of the Marks," *Nature Neuroscience* 13, no. 11 (2010): 1313–18. See also M. J. Meaney, "Epigenetics and the Biological Definition of Gene × Environment Interactions," *Child Development* 81, no. 1 (2010): 41–79; and B. M. Lester, et al., "Behavioral Epigenetics," *Annals of the New York Academy of Sciences* 1226, no. 1 (2011): 14–33.

6. M. Szyf, "The Early Life Social Environment and DNA Methylation: DNA Methylation Mediating the Long-Term Impact of Social Environments Early in Life," *Epigenetics* 6, no. 8 (2011): 971–78.

7. Moshe Szyf, Patrick McGowan, and Michael J. Meaney, "The Social Environment and the Epigenome," *Environmental and Molecular Mutagenesis* 49, no. 1 (2008): 46–60.

8. There now is voluminous evidence that life experiences of all sorts changes gene expression. Some examples are: D. Mehta et al., "Childhood Maltreatment Is Associated with Distinct Genomic and Epigenetic Profiles in Posttraumatic Stress Disorder," *Proceedings of the National Academy of Sciences of the United States of America* 110, no. 20 (2013): 8302–7; P. O. McGowan, et al., "Epigenetic Regulation of the Glucocorticoid Receptor in Human Brain Associates with Childhood Abuse," *Nature Neuroscience* 12, no. 3 (2009): 342–48; M. N. Davies, et al., "Functional Annotation of the Human Brain Methylome Identifies Tissue-Specific Epigenetic Variation Across Brain and Blood," *Genome Biology* 13, no. 6 (2012): R43; M. Gunnar and K. Quevedo, "The Neurobiology of Stress and Development," *Annual Review of Psychology* 58 (2007): 145–73; A. Sommershof, et al., "Substantial Reduction of Naïve and Regulatory T Cells Following Traumatic Stress," *Brain, Behavior, and Immunity* 23, no. 8 (2009): 1117–24; N. Provençal, et al., "The Signature of Maternal Rearing in the Methylome in Rhesus Macaque Prefrontal Cortex and T Cells," *Journal of Neuroscience* 32, no. 44 (2012): 15626–42; B. Labonté, et al., "Genome-wide Epigenetic Regulation by Early-Life Trauma," *Archives of General Psychiatry* 69, no. 7 (2012): 722–31; A. K. Smith, et al., "Differential Immune System DNA Methylation and Cytokine Regulation in Posttraumatic Stress Disorder," *American Journal of Medical Genetics Part B: Neuropsychiatric Genetics* 156B, no. 6 (2011): 700–708; M. Uddin, et al., "Epigenetic and Immune Function Profiles Associated with Posttraumatic Stress Disorder," *Proceedings of the National Academy of Sciences of the United States of America* 107, no. 20 (2010): 9470–75.

9. C. S. Barr, et al., "The Utility of the Non-human Primate Model for Studying Gene by Environment Interactions in Behavioral Research," *Genes, Brain and Behavior* 2, no. 6 (2003): 336–40.

10. A. J. Bennett, et al., "Early Experience and Serotonin Transporter Gene Variation Interact to Influence Primate CNS Function," *Molecular Psychiatry* 7, no. 1 (2002): 118–22. See also C. S. Barr, et al., "Interaction Between Serotonin Transporter Gene Variation and Rearing Condition in Alcohol

Preference and Consumption in Female Primates," *Archives of General Psychiatry* 61, no. 11 (2004): 1146; and C. S. Barr, et al., "Serotonin Transporter Gene Variation Is Associated with Alcohol Sensitivity in Rhesus Macaques Exposed to Early-Life Stress," *Alcoholism: Clinical and Experimental Research* 27, no. 5 (2003): 812–17.

11. A. Roy, et al., "Interaction of FKBP5, a Stress-Related Gene, with Childhood Trauma Increases the Risk for Attempting Suicide," *Neuropsychopharmacology* 35, no. 8 (2010): 1674–83. See also M. A. Enoch, et al., "The Influence of GABRA2, Childhood Trauma, and Their Interaction on Alcohol, Heroin, and Cocaine Dependence," *Biological Psychiatry* 67 no. 1 (2010): 20–27; and A. Roy, et al., "Two HPA Axis Genes, CRHBP and FKBP5, Interact with Childhood Trauma to Increase the Risk for Suicidal Behavior," *Journal of Psychiatric Research* 46, no. 1 (2012): 72–79.

12. A. S. Masten and D. Cicchetti, "Developmental Cascades," *Development and Psychopathology* 22, no. 3 (2010): 491–95; S. L. Toth, et al., "Illogical Thinking and Thought Disorder in Maltreated Children," *Journal of the American Academy of Child & Adolescent Psychiatry* 50, no. 7 (2011): 659–68; J. Willis, "Building a Bridge from Neuroscience to the Classroom," *Phi Delta Kappan* 89, no. 6 (2008): 424; I. M. Eigsti and D. Cicchetti, "The Impact of Child Maltreatment on Expressive Syntax at 60 Months," *Developmental Science* 7, no. 1 (2004): 88–102.

13. J. Spinazzola, et al., "Survey Evaluates Complex Trauma Exposure, Outcome, and Intervention Among Children and Adolescents," *Psychiatric Annals* 35, no. 5 (2005): 433–39.

14. R. C. Kessler, C. B. Nelson, and K. A. McGonagle, "The Epidemiology of Co-occuring Addictive and Mental Disorders," *American Journal of Orthopsychiatry* 66, no. 1 (1996): 17–31. See also Institute of Medicine of the National Academies, *Treatment of Posttraumatic Stress Disorder* (Washington: National Academies Press, 2008); and C. S. North, et al., "Toward Validation of the Diagnosis of Posttraumatic Stress Disorder," *American Journal of Psychiatry* 166, no. 1 (2009): 34–40.

15. Joseph Spinazzola, et al., "Survey Evaluates Complex Trauma Exposure, Outcome, and Intervention Among Children and Adolescents," *Psychiatric Annals* (2005).

16. Our work group consisted of Drs. Bob Pynoos, Frank Putnam, Glenn Saxe, Julian Ford, Joseph Spinazzola, Marylene Cloitre, Bradley Stolbach, Alexander McFarlane, Alicia Lieberman, Wendy D'Andrea, Martin Teicher, and Dante Cicchetti.

17. The proposed criteria for Developmental Trauma Disorder can be found in the Appendix.

18. http://www.traumacenter.org/products/instruments.php.

19. Read more about Sroufe at www.cehd.umn.edu/icd/people/faculty/cpsy/sroufe.html and more about the Minnesota Longitudinal Study of Risk and Adaptation and its publications at http://www.cehd.umn.edu/icd/research/parent-child/ and http://www.cehd.umn.edu/icd/research/parent-child/publications/. See also L. A. Sroufe and W. A. Collins, *The Development of the Person: The Minnesota Study of Risk and Adaptation from Birth to Adulthood* (New York: Guilford Press, 2009); and L. A. Sroufe, "Attachment and Development: A Prospective, Longitudinal Study from Birth to Adulthood," *Attachment & Human Development* 7, no. 4 (2005): 349–67.

20. L. A. Sroufe, *The Development of the Person: The Minnesota Study of Risk and Adaptation from Birth to Adulthood* (New York: Guilford Press, 2005). Harvard researcher Karlen Lyons-Ruth had similar findings in a sample of children she followed for about eighteen years: Disorganized attachment, role reversal, and lack of maternal communication at age three were the greatest predictors of children being part of the mental health or social service system at age eighteen.

21. D. Jacobvitz and L. A. Sroufe, "The Early Caregiver-Child Relationship and Attention-Deficit Disorder with Hyperactivity in Kindergarten: A Prospective Study," *Child Development* 58, no. 6 (December 1987): 1496–504.

22. G. H. Elder Jr., T. Van Nguyen, and A. Caspi, "Linking Family Hardship to Children's Lives," *Child Development* 56, no. 2 (April 1985): 361–75.

23. For children who were physically abused, the chance of being diagnosed with conduct disorder or oppositional defiant disorder went up by a factor of three. Neglect or sexual abuse doubled the chance

of developing an anxiety disorder. Parental psychological unavailability or sexual abuse doubled the chance of later developing PTSD. The chance of receiving multiple diagnoses was 54 percent for children who suffered neglect, 60 percent for physical abuse, and 73 percent for both sexual abuse.

24. This was a quote based on the work of Emmy Werner, who has studied 698 children born on the island of Kauai for forty years, starting in 1955. The study showed that most children who grew up in unstable households grew up to experience problems with delinquency, mental and physical health, and family stability. One-third of all high-risk children displayed resilience and developed into caring, competent, and confident adults. *Protective factors* were 1. being an appealing child, 2. a strong bond with a nonparent caretaker (such as an aunt, a babysitter, or a teacher) and strong involvement in church or community groups. E. E. Werner and R. S. Smith, *Overcoming the Odds: High Risk Children from Birth to Adulthood* (Ithaca and London: Cornell University Press, 1992).

25. P. K. Trickett, J. G. Noll, and F. W. Putnam, "The Impact of Sexual Abuse on Female Development: Lessons from a Multigenerational, Longitudinal Research Study," *Development and Psychopathology* 23 (2011): 453–76. See also J. G. Noll, P. K. Trickett, and F. W. Putnam, "A Prospective Investigation of the Impact of Childhood Sexual Abuse on the Development of Sexuality," *Journal of Consulting and Clinical Psychology* 71 (2003): 575–86; P. K. Trickett, C. McBride-Chang, and F. W. Putnam, "The Classroom Performance and Behavior of Sexually Abused Females," *Development and Psychopathology* 6 (1994): 183–94; P. K. Trickett and F. W. Putnam, *Sexual Abuse of Females: Effects in Childhood* (Washington: National Institute of Mental Health, 1990–1993); F. W. Putnam and P. K. Trickett, *The Psychobiological Effects of Child Sexual Abuse* (New York: W. T. Grant Foundation, 1987).

26. In the sixty-three studies on disruptive mood regulation disorder, nobody asked anything about attachment, PTSD, trauma, child abuse, or neglect. The word "maltreatment" is used in passing in just one of the sixty-three articles. There is nothing about parenting, family dynamics, or about family therapy.

27. In the appendix at the back of the DSM, you can find the so-called V-codes, diagnostic labels without official standing that are not eligible for insurance reimbursement. There you will see listings for childhood abuse, childhood neglect, childhood physical abuse, and childhood sexual abuse.

28. Ibid., p 121.

29. At the time of this writing, the DSM-5 is number seven on Amazon's best-seller list. The APA earned $100 million on the previous edition of the DSM. The publication of the DSM constitutes, with contributions from the pharmaceutical industry and membership dues, the APA's major source of income.

30. Gary Greenberg, *The Book of Woe: The DSM and the Unmaking of Psychiatry* (New York: Penguin, 2013), 239.

31. In an open letter to the APA David Elkins, the chairman of one of the divisions of the American Psychological Association, complained that DSM-V was based on shaky evidence, carelessness with the public health, and the conceptualizations of mental disorder as primarily medical phenomena." His letter attracted nearly five thousand signatures. The president of the American Counseling Association sent a letter on behalf of its 115,000 DSM-buying members to the president of the APA, also objecting to the quality of the science behind DSM-5—and "urge(d) the APA to make public the work of the scientific review committee it had appointed to review the proposed changes, as well as to allow an evaluation of "all evidence and data by external, independent groups of experts."

32. Thomas Insel had formerly done research on the attachment hormone oxytocin in non-human primates.

33. National Institute of Mental Health, "NIMH Research Domain Criteria (RDoC)," http://www.nimh.nih.gov/research-priorities/rdoc/nimh-research-domain-criteria-rdoc.shtml.

34. *The Development of the Person: The Minnesota Study of Risk and Adaptation from Birth to Adulthood* (New York: Guilford Press, 2005).

35. B. A. van der Kolk, "Developmental Trauma Disorder: Toward a Rational Diagnosis for Children

with Complex Trauma Histories," *Psychiatric Annals* 35, no. 5 (2005): 401–8; W. D'Andrea, et al., "Understanding Interpersonal Trauma in Children: Why We Need a Developmentally Appropriate Trauma Diagnosis," *American Journal of Orthopsychiatry* 82 (2012): 187–200. J. D. Ford, et al., "Clinical Significance of a Proposed Developmental Trauma Disorder Diagnosis: Results of an International Survey of Clinicians," *Journal of Clinical Psychiatry* 74, no. 8 (2013): 841–849. Up-to-date results from the Developmental Trauma Disorder field trial study are available on our Web site: www.traumacenter.org.

36. J. J. Heckman, "Skill Formation and the Economics of Investing in Disadvantaged Children," *Science* 312, no. 5782 (2006): 1900–2.

37. D. Olds, et al., "Long-Term Effects of Nurse Home Visitation on Children's Criminal and Antisocial Behavior: 15-Year Follow-up of a Randomized Controlled Trial," *JAMA* 280, no. 14 (1998): 1238–44. See also J. Eckenrode, et al., "Preventing Child Abuse and Neglect with a Program of Nurse Home Visitation: The Limiting Effects of Domestic Violence," *JAMA* 284, no. 11 (2000): 1385–91; D. I. Lowell, et al., "A Randomized Controlled Trial of Child FIRST: A Comprehensive Home-Based Intervention Translating Research into Early Childhood Practice," *Child Development* 82, no. 1 (January/February 2011): 193–208; S. T. Harvey and J. E. Taylor, "A Meta-Analysis of the Effects of Psychotherapy with Sexually Abused Children and Adolescents, *Clinical Psychology Review* 30, no. 5 (July 2010): 517–35; J. E. Taylor and S. T. Harvey, "A Meta-Analysis of the Effects of Psychotherapy with Adults Sexually Abused in Childhood," *Clinical Psychology Review* 30, no. 6 (August 2010): 749–67; Olds, Henderson, Chamberlin, & Tatelbaum, 1986; B. C. Stolbach, et al., "Complex Trauma Exposure and Symptoms in Urban Traumatized Children: A Preliminary Test of Proposed Criteria for Developmental Trauma Disorder," *Journal of Traumatic Stress* 26, no. 4 (August 2013): 483–91.

CHAPTER 11: UNCOVERING SECRETS: THE PROBLEM OF TRAUMATIC MEMORY

1. Unlike clinical consultations, in which doctor-patient confidentiality applies, forensic evaluations are public documents to be shared with lawyers, courts, and juries. Before doing a forensic evaluation I inform clients of that and warn them that nothing they tell me can be kept confidential.

2. K. A. Lee, et al., "A 50-Year Prospective Study of the Psychological Sequelae of World War II Combat," *American Journal of Psychiatry* 152, no. 4 (April 1995): 516–22.

3. J. L. McGaugh and M. L. Hertz, *Memory Consolidation* (San Fransisco: Albion Press, 1972); L. Cahill and J. L. McGaugh, "Mechanisms of Emotional Arousal and Lasting Declarative Memory," *Trends in Neurosciences* 21, no. 7 (1998): 294–99.

4. A. F. Arnsten, et al., "α-1 Noradrenergic Receptor Stimulation Impairs Prefrontal Cortical Cognitive Function," *Biological Psychiatry* 45, no. 1 (1999): 26–31. See also A. F. Arnsten, "Enhanced: The Biology of Being Frazzled," *Science* 280, no. 5370 (1998): 1711–12; S. Birnbaum, et al., "A Role for Norepinephrine in Stress-Induced Cognitive Deficits: α-1-adrenoceptor Mediation in the Prefrontal Cortex," *Biological Psychiatry* 46, no. 9 (1999): 1266–74.

5. Y. D. Van Der Werf, *et al.* "Special Issue: Contributions of Thalamic Nuclei to Declarative Memory Functioning," *Cortex* 39 (2003): 1047–62. See also B. M. Elzinga and J. D. Bremner, "Are the Neural Substrates of Memory the Final Common Pathway in Posttraumatic Stress Disorder (PTSD)?" *Journal of Affective Disorders* 70 (2002): 1–17; L. M. Shin et al., "A Functional Magnetic Resonance Imaging Study of Amygdala and Medial Prefrontal Cortex Responses to Overtly Presented Fearful Faces in Posttraumatic Stress Disorder," *Archives of General Psychiatry* 62 (2005): 273–81; L. M. Williams et al., "Trauma Modulates Amygdala and Medial Prefrontal Responses to Consciously Attended Fear," *Neuroimage* 29 (2006): 347–57; R. A. Lanius et al., "Brain Activation During Script-Driven Imagery Induced Dissociative Responses in PTSD: A Functional Magnetic Resonance Imaging Investigation," *Biological Psychiatry* 52 (2002): 305–311; H. D Critchley, C. J. Mathias, and R. J. Dolan, "Fear Conditioning in Humans: The Influence of Awareness and Autonomic Arousal on Functional Neuroanatomy," *Neuron* 33 (2002): 653–63; M. Beauregard, J. Levesque, and P. Bourgouin, "Neural

Correlates of Conscious Self-Regulation of Emotion," *Journal of Neuroscience* 21 (2001): RC165; K. N. Ochsner et al., "For Better or for Worse: Neural Systems Supporting the Cognitive Down-and Up-Regulation of Negative Emotion," *NeuroImage* 23 (2004): 483–99; M. A. Morgan, L. M. Romanski, and J. E. LeDoux, et al., "Extinction of Emotional Learning: Contribution of Medial Prefrontal Cortex," *Neuroscience Letters* 163 (1993): 109–13; M. R. Milad and G. J. Quirk, "Neurons in Medial Prefrontal Cortex Signal Memory for Fear Extinction," *Nature* 420 (2002): 70–74; and J. Amat, et al., "Medial Prefrontal Cortex Determines How Stressor Controllability Affects Behavior and Dorsal Raphe Nucleus," *Nature Neuroscience* 8 (2005): 365–71.

6. B. A. Van der Kolk and R. Fisler, "Dissociation and the Fragmentary Nature of Traumatic Memories: Overview and Exploratory Study," *Journal of Traumatic Stress* 8, no. 4 (1995): 505–25.

7. Hysteria as defined by Free Dictionary, http://www.thefreedictionary.com/hysteria.

8. A. Young, *The Harmony of Illusions: Inventing Posttraumatic Stress Disorder* (Princeton University Press, 1997). See also H. F. Ellenberger, *The Discovery of the Unconscious: The History and Evolution of Dynamic Psychiatry* (Basic Books, 2008).

9. T. Ribot, *Diseases of Memory* (Appleton, 1887), 108–9; Ellenberger, *Discovery of the Unconscious.*

10. J. Breuer and S. Freud, "The Physical Mechanisms of Hysterical Phenomena," in *The Standard Edition of the Complete Psychological Works of Sigmund Freud* (London: Hogarth Press, 1893).

11. A. Young, *Harmony of Illusions.*

12. J. L. Herman, *Trauma and Recovery* (New York: Basic Books, 1997), 15.

13. A. Young, *Harmony of Illusions.* See also J. M. Charcot, *Clinical Lectures on Certain Diseases of the Nervous System,* vol. 3 (London: New Sydenham Society, 1888).

14. http://en.wikipedia.org/wiki/File:Jean-Martin_Charcot_chronophotography.jpg

15. P. Janet, *L'Automatisme psychologique* (Paris: Félix Alcan, 1889).

16. Onno van der Hart introduced me to the work of Janet and probably is the greatest living scholar of his work. I had the good fortune of closely collaborating with Onno on summarizing Janet's fundamental ideas. B. A. van der Kolk and O. van der Hart, "Pierre Janet and the Breakdown of Adaptation in Psychological Trauma," *American Journal of Psychiatry* 146 (1989): 1530–40; B. A. van der Kolk and O. van der Hart, "The Intrusive Past: The Flexibility of Memory and the Engraving of Trauma," *Imago* 48 (1991): 425–54.

17. P. Janet, "L'amnésie et la dissociation des souvenirs par l'emotion" [Amnesia and the dissociation of memories by emotions], *Journal de Psychologie* 1 (1904): 417–53.

18. P. Janet, *Psychological Healing* (New York: Macmillan, 1925); p 660.

19. P. Janet, *L'Etat mental des hystériques,* 2nd ed. (Paris: Félix Alcan, 1911; repr. Marseille, France: Lafitte Reprints, 1983). P. Janet, *The Major Symptoms of Hysteria* (London and New York: Macmillan, 1907; repr. New York: Hafner, 1965); P. Janet, *L'evolution de la memoire et de la notion du temps* (Paris: A. Chahine, 1928).

20. J. L. Titchener, "Posttraumatic Decline: A Consequence of Unresolved Destructive Drives," *Trauma and Its Wake 2* (1986): 5–19.

21. J. Breuer, and S. Freud, "The Physical Mechanisms of Hysterical Phenomena."

22. S. Freud and J. Breuer, "The Etiology of Hysteria," in the *Standard Edition of the Complete Psychological Works of Sigmund Freud,* vol. 3, ed. J. Strachy (London: Hogarth Press, 1962): 189–221.

23. S. Freud, "Three Essays on the Theory of Sexuality," in the *Standard Edition of the Complete Psychological Works of Sigmund Freud,* vol. 7 (London: Hogarth Press, 1962): 190: The reappearance of sexual activity is determined by internal causes and external contingencies . . . I shall have to speak presently of the internal causes; *great and lasting importance attaches at this period to the accidental external* [Freud's emphasis] *contingencies. In the foreground we find the effects of seduction, which treats a child as a sexual object prematurely* and teaches him, in highly emotional circumstances, how to obtain satisfaction from his genital zones, a satisfaction which he is then usually obliged to repeat again and again by masturbation. An influence of this kind may originate either from adults or from

other children. *I cannot admit that in my paper on 'The Aetiology of Hysteria' (1896c) I exaggerated the frequency or importance of that influence*, though I did not then know that persons who remain normal may have had the same experiences in their childhood, and though I consequently overrated the importance of seduction in comparison with the factors of sexual constitution and development. Obviously seduction is not required in order to arouse a child's sexual life; that can also come about spontaneously from internal causes. S. Freud "Introductory Lectures in Psychoanalysis in *Stand ard Edition* (1916), 370: Phantasies of being seduced are of particular interest, because so often they are not phantasies but real memories.

24. S. Freud, *Inhibitions Symptoms and Anxiety* (1914), 150. See also Strachey, *Standard Edition of the Complete Psychological Works*.

25. B. A. van der Kolk, *Psychological Trauma* (Washington, D: American Psychiatric Press, 1986).

26. B. A. Van der Kolk, "The Compulsion to Repeat the Trauma," *Psychiatric Clinics of North America* 12, no. 2 (1989): 389–411.

CHAPTER 12: THE UNBEARABLE HEAVINESS OF REMEMBERING

1. A. Young, *The Harmony of Illusions: Inventing Posttraumatic Stress Disorder* (Princeton, NJ: Princeton University Press, 1997), 84.

2. F. W. Mott, "Special Discussion on Shell Shock Without Visible Signs of Injury," *Proceedings of the Royal Society of Medicine* 9 (1916): i–xliv. See also C. S. Myers, "A Contribution to the Study of Shell Shock," *Lancet* 1 (1915): 316–20; T. W. Salmon, "The Care and Treatment of Mental Diseases and War Neuroses ("Shell Shock") in the British Army," *Mental Hygiene* 1 (1917): 509–47; and E. Jones and S. Wessely, *Shell Shock to PTSD: Military Psychiatry from 1900 to the Gulf* (Hove, UK: Psychology Press, 2005).

3. J. Keegan, *The First World War* (New York: Random House, 2011).

4. A. D. Macleod, "Shell Shock, Gordon Holmes and the Great War." *Journal of the Royal Society of Medicine* 97, no. 2 (2004): 86–89; M. Eckstein, *Rites of Spring: The Great War and the Birth of the Modern Age* (Boston: Houghton Mifflin, 1989).

5. Lord Southborough, *Report of the War Office Committee of Enquiry into "Shell-Shock"* (London: His Majesty's Stationery Office, 1922).

6. Booker Prize winner Pat Barker has written a moving trilogy about the work of army psychiatrist W. H. R. Rivers: P. Barker, *Regeneration* (London: Penguin UK, 2008); P. Barker, *The Eye in the Door* (New York: Penguin, 1995); P. Barker, *The Ghost Road* (London: Penguin UK, 2008). Further discussions of the aftermath of World War I can be found in *A. Young, Harmony of Illusions;* and B. Shephard, *A War of Nerves, Soldiers and Psychiatrists 1914–1994* (London: Jonathan Cape, 2000).

7. J. H. Bartlett, *The Bonus March and the New Deal* (1937); R. Daniels, T*he Bonus March: An Episode of the Great Depression* (1971).

8. E. M. Remarque, *All Quiet on the Western Front*, trans. A. W. Wheen (London: GP Putnam's Sons, 1929).

9. Ibid., pp. 192–93.

10. For an account, see http://motlc.wiesenthal.com/site/pp.asp?c=gvKVLcMVIuG&b=395007.

11. C. S. Myers, *Shell Shock in France 1914–1918* (Cambridge UK, Cambridge University Press, 1940).

12. A. Kardiner, *The Traumatic Neuroses of War* (New York: Hoeber, 1941).

13. http://en.wikipedia.org/wiki/Let_There_Be_Light_(film).

14. G. Greer and J. Oxenbould, *Daddy, We Hardly Knew You* (London: Penguin, 1990).

15. A. Kardiner and H. Spiegel, *War Stress and Neurotic Illness* (Oxford, England: Hoeber, 1947).

16. D. J. Henderson, "Incest," in *Comprehensive Textbook of Psychiatry*, 2nd ed., eds. A. M. Freedman and H. I. Kaplan (Baltimore: Williams & Wilkins, 1974), p. 1536.

17. W. Sargent and E. Slater, "Acute War Neuroses," *The Lancet* 236, no. 6097 (1940): 1–2. See also G. Debenham, et al., "Treatment of War Neurosis," *The Lancet* 237, no. 6126 (1941): 107–9; and W.

Sargent and E. Slater, "Amnesic Syndromes in War," *Proceedings of the Royal Society of Medicine* (Section of Psychiatry) 34, no. 12 (October 1941): 757–64.

18. Every single scientific study of memory of childhood sexual abuse, whether prospective or retrospective, whether studying clinical samples or general population samples, finds that a certain percentage of sexually abused individuals forget, and later remember, their abuse. See, e.g., B. A. van der Kolk and R. Fisler, "Dissociation and the Fragmentary Nature of Traumatic Memories: Overview and Exploratory Study," *Journal of Traumatic Stress* 8 (1995): 505–25; J. W. Hopper and B. A. van der Kolk, "Retrieving, Assessing, and Classifying Traumatic Memories: A Preliminary Report on Three Case Studies of a New Standardized Method," *Journal of Aggression, Maltreatment & Trauma* 4 (2001): 33–71; J. J. Freyd and A. P. DePrince, eds., *Trauma and Cognitive Science* (Binghamton, NY: Haworth Press, 2001), 33–71; A. P. DePrince and J. J. Freyd, "The Meeting of Trauma and Cognitive Science: Facing Challenges and Creating Opportunities at the Crossroads," *Journal of Aggression, Maltreatment & Trauma* 4, no. 2 (2001): 1–8; D. Brown, A. W. Scheflin, and D. Corydon Hammond, *Memory, Trauma Treatment and the Law* (New York: Norton, 1997); K. Pope and L. Brown, *Recovered Memories of Abuse: Assessment, Therapy, Forensics* (Washington: American Psychological Association, 1996); and L. Terr, *Unchained Memories: True Stories of Traumatic Memories, Lost and Found* (New York: Basic Books, 1994).

19. E. F. Loftus, S. Polonsky, and M. T. Fullilove, "Memories of Childhood Sexual Abuse: Remembering and Repressing," *Psychology of Women Quarterly* 18, no. 1 (1994): 67–84. L. M. Williams, "Recall of Childhood Trauma: A Prospective Study of Women's Memories of Child Sexual Abuse," *Journal of Consulting and Clinical Psychology* 62, no. 6 (1994): 1167–76.

20. L. M. Williams, "Recall of Childhood Trauma."

21. L. M. Williams, "Recovered Memories of Abuse in Women with Documented Child Sexual Victimization Histories," *Journal of Traumatic Stress* 8, no. 4 (1995): 649–73.

22. The prominent neuroscientist Jaak Panksepp states in his most recent book: "Abundant preclinical work with animal models has now shown that memories that are retrieved tend to return to their memory banks with modifications." J. Panksepp and L. Biven, *The Archaeology of Mind: Neuroevolutionary Origins of Human Emotions*, Norton Series on Interpersonal Neurobiology (New York: WW Norton, 2012).

23. E. F. Loftus, "The Reality of Repressed Memories," *American Psychologist* 48, no. 5 (1993): 518–37. See also E. F. Loftus and K. Ketcham, *The Myth of Repressed Memory: False Memories and Allegations of Sexual Abuse* (New York: Macmillan, 1996).

24. J. F. Kihlstrom, "The Cognitive Unconscious," *Science* 237, no. 4821 (1987): 1445–52.

25. E. F. Loftus, "Planting Misinformation in the Human Mind: A 30-Year Investigation of the Malleability of Memory," *Learning & Memory* 12, no. 4 (2005): 361–66.

26. B. A. Van der Kolk and R. Fisler, "Dissociation and the Fragmentary Nature of Traumatic Memories: Overview and Exploratory Study," *Journal of Traumatic Stress* 8, no. 4 (1995): 505–25.

27. We will explore this further in chapter 14.

28. L. L. Langer, *Holocaust Testimonies: The Ruins of Memory* (New Haven: Yale University Press, 1991).

29. Ibid., p.5.

30. L. L. Langer, op cit., p. 21.

31. L. L. Langer, op cit., p. 34.

32. J. Osterman and B. A. van der Kolk, "Awareness during Anaesthesia and Posttraumatic Stress Disorder," *General Hospital Psychiatry* 20 (1998): 274-81. See also K. Kiviniemi, "Conscious Awareness and Memory During General Anesthesia," *Journal of the American Association of Nurse Anesthetists* 62 (1994): 441–49; A. D. Macleod and E. Maycock, "Awareness During Anaesthesia and Post Traumatic Stress Disorder," *Anaesthesia and Intensive Care* 20, no. 3 (1992) 378–82; F. Guerra, "Awareness and Recall: Neurological and Psychological Complications of Surgery and Anesthesia," in *International Anesthesiology Clinics, vol. 24.* ed. B. T Hindman (Boston: Little Brown, 1986), 75–99;

J. Eldor and D. Z. N. Frankel, "Intra-anesthetic Awareness," *Resuscitation* 21 (1991): 113–19; J. L. Breckenridge and A. R. Aitkenhead, "Awareness During Anaesthesia: A Review," *Annals of the Royal College of Surgeons of England* 65, no. 2 (1983), 93.

CHAPTER 13: HEALING FROM TRAUMA: OWNING YOUR SELF

1. "Self-leadership" is the term used by Dick Schwartz in internal family system therapy, the topic of chapter 17.
2. The exceptions are Pesso's and Schwartz's work, detailed in chapters 17 and 18, which I practice, and from which I have personally benefited, but which I have not studied scientifically—at least not yet.
3. A. F. Arnsten, "Enhanced: The Biology of Being Frazzled," *Science* 280, no. 5370 (1998): 1711–12; A. Arnsten, "Stress Signalling Pathways That Impair Prefrontal Cortex Structure and Function," *Nature Reviews Neuroscience* 10, no. 6 (2009): 410–22.
4. D. J. Siegel, *The Mindful Therapist: A Clinician's Guide to Mindsight and Neural Integration* (New York: WW Norton, 2010).
5. J. E. LeDoux, "Emotion Circuits in the Brain," *Annual Review of Neuroscience* 23, no. 1 (2000): 155–84. See also M. A. Morgan, L. M. Romanski, and J. E. LeDoux, "Extinction of Emotional Learning: Contribution of Medial Prefrontal Cortex," *Neuroscience Letters* 163, no. 1 (1993): 109–113; and J. M. Moscarello and J. E. LeDoux, "Active Avoidance Learning Requires Prefrontal Suppression of Amygdala-Mediated Defensive Reactions," *Journal of Neuroscience* 33, no. 9 (2013): 3815–23.
6. S. W. Porges, "Stress and Parasympathetic Control," *Stress Science: Neuroendocrinology* 306 (2010). See also S. W. Porges, "Reciprocal Influences Between Body and Brain in the Perception and Expression of Affect," in *The Healing Power of Emotion: Affective Neuroscience, Development & Clinical Practice*, Norton Series on Interpersonal Neurobiology (New York: WW Norton, 2009), 27.
7. B. A. van der Kolk, et al., "Yoga As an Adjunctive Treatment for PTSD." *Journal of Clinical Psychiatry* 75, no. 6 (June 2014): 559–65.
8. Sebern F. Fisher, *Neurofeedback in the Treatment of Developmental Trauma: Calming the Fear-Driven Brain*. (New York: WW Norton & Company, 2014).
9. R. P. Brown and P. L. Gerbarg, "Sudarshan Kriya Yogic Breathing in the Treatment of Stress, Anxiety, and Depression—Part II: Clinical Applications and Guidelines," *Journal of Alternative & Complementary Medicine* 11, no. 4 (2005): 711–17. See also C. L. Mandle, et al., "The Efficacy of Relaxation Response Interventions with Adult Patients: A Review of the Literature," *Journal of Cardiovascular Nursing* 10 (1996): 4–26; and M. Nakao, et al., "Anxiety Is a Good Indicator for Somatic Symptom Reduction Through Behavioral Medicine Intervention in a Mind/Body Medicine Clinic," *Psychotherapy and Psychosomatics* 70 (2001): 50–57.
10. C. Hannaford, *Smart Moves: Why Learning Is Not All in Your Head* (Arlington, VA: Great Ocean Publishers, 1995), 22207–3746.
11. J. Kabat-Zinn, *Full Catastrophe Living: Using the Wisdom of Your Body and Mind to Face Stress, Pain, and Illness* (New York: Bantam Books, 2013). See also D. Fosha, D. J. Siegel, and M. Solomon, eds., *The Healing Power of Emotion: Affective Neuroscience, Development & Clinical Practice*, Norton Series on Interpersonal Neurobiology (New York: WW Norton, 2011); and B. A. van der Kolk, "Posttraumatic Therapy in the Age of Neuroscience," *Psychoanalytic Dialogues* 12, no. 3 (2002): 381–92.
12. As we have seen in chapter 5, brain scans of people suffering from PTSD show altered activation in areas associated with the default network, which is involved with autobiographical memory and a continuous sense of self.
13. P. A. Levine, *In an Unspoken Voice: How the Body Releases Trauma and Restores Goodness* (Berkeley: North Atlantic, 2010).
14. P. Ogden, *Trauma and the Body* (New York: Norton, 2009). See also A. Y. Shalev, "Measuring Outcome in Posttraumatic Stress Disorder," *Journal of Clinical Psychiatry* 61, supp. 5 (2000): 33–42.

15. I. Kabat-Zinn, *Full Catastrophe Living*. p. xx

16. S. G. Hofmann, et al., "The Effect of Mindfulness-Based Therapy on Anxiety and Depression: A Meta-Analytic Review," *Journal of Consulting and Clinical Psychology* 78, no.2 (2010): 169–83; J. D. Teasdale, et al., "Prevention of Relapse/Recurrence in Major Depression by Mindfulness-Based Cognitive Therapy," *Journal of Consulting and Clinical Psychology* 68 (2000): 615–23. See also Britta K. Hölzel, et al., "How Does Mindfulness Meditation Work? Proposing Mechanisms of Action from a Conceptual and Neural Perspective." *Perspectives on Psychological Science* 6, no. 6 (2011): 537–59; and P. Grossman, et al., "Mindfulness-Based Stress Reduction and Health Benefits: A Meta-Analysis," *Journal of Psychosomatic Research* 57, no. 1 (2004): 35–43.

17. The brain circuits involved in mindfulness meditation have been well established, and improve attention regulation and has a positive effect on the interference of emotional reactions with attentional performance tasks. See L. E. Carlson, et al., "One Year Pre-Post Intervention Follow-up of Psychological, Immune, Endocrine and Blood Pressure Outcomes of Mindfulness-Based Stress Reduction (MBSR) in Breast and Prostate Cancer Outpatients," *Brain, Behavior, and Immunity* 21, no. 8 (2007): 1038–49; and R. J. Davidson, et al., "Alterations in Brain and Immune Function Produced by Mindfulness Meditation," Psychosomatic Medicine 65, no. 4 (2003): 564–70.

18. Britta Hölzel and her colleagues have done extensive research on meditation and brain function and have shown that it involves the dorsomedial PFC, ventrolateral PFC, and rostral anterior congulate (ACC). See B. K. Hölzel, et al., "Stress Reduction Correlates with Structural Changes in the Amygdala," *Social Cognitive and Affective Neuroscience* 5 (2010): 11–17; B. K. Hölzel, et al., "Mindfulness Practice Leads to Increases in Regional Brain Gray Matter Density," *Psychiatry Research* 191, no. 1 (2011): 36–43; B. K. Hölzel, et al., "Investigation of Mindfulness Meditation Practitioners with Voxel-Based Morphometry," *Social Cognitive and Affective Neuroscience* 3, no. 1 (2008): 55–61; and B. K. Hölzel, et al., "Differential Engagement of Anterior Cingulate and Adjacent Medial Frontal Cortex in Adept Meditators and Non-meditators," *Neuroscience Letters* 421, no. 1 (2007): 16–21.

19. The main brain structure involved in body awareness is the anterior insula. See A. D. Craig, "Interoception: The Sense of the Physiological Condition of the Body," *Current Opinion on Neurobiology* 13 (2003): 500–505; Critchley, Wiens, Rotshtein, Ohman, and Dolan, 2004; N. A. S Farb, Z. V. Segal, H. Mayberg, J. Bean, D. McKeon, Z. Fatima, et al., "Attending to the Present: Mindfulness Meditation Reveals Distinct Neural Modes of Self-Reference," *Social Cognitive and Affective Neuroscience* 2 (2007): 313–22.; J. A. Grant, J. Courtemanche, E. G. Duerden, G. H. Duncan, and P. Rainville, (2010). "Cortical Thickness and Pain Sensitivity in Zen Meditators," *Emotion* 10, no. 1 (2010): 43–53.

20. S. J. Banks, et al., "Amygdala-Frontal Connectivity During Emotion-Regulation," *Social Cognitive and Affective Neuroscience* 2, no. 4 (2007): 303–12. See also M. R. Milad, et al., "Thickness of Ventromedial Prefrontal Cortex in Humans Is Correlated with Extinction Memory," *Proceedings of the National Academy of Sciences of the United States of America* 102, no. 30 (2005): 10706–11; and S. L. Rauch, L. M. Shin, and E. A. Phelps, "Neurocircuitry Models of Posttraumatic Stress Disorder and Extinction: Human Neuroimaging Research—Past, Present, and Future," *Biological Psychiatry* 60, no. 4 (2006): 376–82.

21. A. Freud and D. T. Burlingham. *War and Children* (New York University Press, 1943).

22. There are three different ways in which people deal with overwhelming experiences: dissociation (spacing out, shutting down), depersonalization (feeling like it's not you it's happening to), and derealization (feeling like whatever is happening is not real).

23. My colleagues at the Justice Resource Institute created a residential treatment program for adolescents, The van der Kolk Center at Glenhaven Academy, that implements many of the trauma-informed treatments discussed in this book, including yoga, sensory integration, neurofeedback and theater. http://www.jri.org/vanderkolk/about. The overarching treatment model, attachment, self-regulation, and competency (ARC), was developed by my colleagues Margaret Blaustein and Kristine

Kinneburgh. Margaret E. Blaustein, and Kristine M. Kinniburgh, *Treating Traumatic Stress in Children and Adolescents: How to Foster Resilience Through Attachment, Self-Regulation, and Competency* (New York: Guilford Press, 2012).

24. C. K. Chandler, *Animal Assisted Therapy in Counseling* (New York: Routledge, 2011). See also A. J. Cleveland, "Therapy Dogs and the Dissociative Patient: Preliminary Observations," *Dissociation* 8, no. 4 (1995): 247–52; and A. Fine, *Handbook on Animal Assisted Therapy: Theoretical Foundations and Guidelines for Practice* (San Diego: Academic Press, 2010).

25. E. Warner, et al., "Can the Body Change the Score? Application of Sensory Modulation Principles in the Treatment of Traumatized Adolescents in Residential Settings," *Journal of Family Violence* 28, no. 7 (2013): 729–38. See also A. J. Ayres, *Sensory Integration and Learning Disorders* (Los Angeles: Western Psychological Services, 1972); H. Hodgdon, et al., "Development and Implementation of Trauma-Informed Programming in Residential Schools Using the ARC Framework," *Journal of Family Violence* 27, no. 8 (2013); J. LeBel, et al., "Integrating Sensory and Trauma-Informed Interventions: A Massachusetts State Initiative, Part 1," *Mental Health Special Interest Section Quarterly* 33, no. 1 (2010): 1–4;

26. They appeared to have activated the vestibule-cerebellar system in the brain, which seems to be involved in self-regulation and can be damaged by early neglect.

27. Aaron R. Lyon and Karen S. Budd, "A Community Mental Health Implementation of Parent–Child Interaction Therapy (PCIT)." *Journal of Child and Family Studies* 19, no. 5 (2010): 654–68. See also Anthony J. Urquiza and Cheryl Bodiford McNeil, "Parent-Child Interaction Therapy: An Intensive Dyadic Intervention for Physically Abusive Families." *Child Maltreatment* 1, no 2 (1996): 134–44; J. Borrego Jr., *et al.* "Research Publications." *Child and Family Behavior Therapy* 20: 27-54.

28. B. A. van der Kolk, et al., "Fluoxetine in Post Traumatic Stress," *Journal of Clinical Psychiatry* (1994): 517–22.

29. P. Ogden, K. Minton, and C. Pain, *Trauma and the Body* (New York, Norton, 2010); P. Ogden and J. Fisher, *Sensorimotor Psychotherapy: Interventions for Trauma and Attachment* (New York: Norton, 2014).

30. P. Levine, *In an Unspoken Voice* (Berkeley: North Atlantic Books); P. Levine, *Waking the Tiger* (Berkeley: North Atlantic Books).

31. For more on impact model mugging, see http://modelmugging.org/.

32. S. Freud, *Remembering, Repeating, and Working Through (Further Recommendations on the Technique of Psychoanalysis II)*, standard ed. (London: Hogarth Press, 1914), p. 371

33. E. Santini, R. U. Muller, and G. J. Quirk, "Consolidation of Extinction Learning Involves Transfer from NMDA-Independent to NMDA-Dependent Memory," *Journal of Neuroscience* 21 (2001): 9009–17.

34. E. B. Foa and M. J. Kozak, "Emotional Processing of Fear: Exposure to Corrective Information," *Psychological Bulletin* 99, no. 1 (1986): 20–35.

35. C. R. Brewin, "Implications for Psychological Intervention," in *Neuropsychology of PTSD: Biological, Cognitive, and Clinical Perspectives*, ed. J. J. Vasterling and C. R. Brewin (New York: Guilford, 2005), 272.

36. T. M. Keane, "The Role of Exposure Therapy in the Psychological Treatment of PTSD," *National Center for PTSD Clinical Quarterly* 5, no. 4 (1995): 1–6.

37. E. B. Foa and R. J. McNally, "Mechanisms of Change in Exposure Therapy," in *Current Controversies in the Anxiety Disorders*, ed. R. M. Rapee (New York: Guilford, 1996), 329–43.

38. J. D. Ford and P. Kidd, "Early Childhood Trauma and Disorders of Extreme Stress as Predictors of Treatment Outcome with Chronic PTSD," *Journal of Traumatic Stress* 18 (1998): 743–61. See also A. McDonagh-Coyle, et al., "Randomized Trial of Cognitive-Behavioral Therapy for Chronic Posttraumatic Stress Disorder in Adult Female Survivors of Childhood Sexual Abuse," *Journal of Consulting and Clinical Psychology* 73, no. 3 (2005): 515–24; Institute of Medicine of the National Academies, *Treatment of Posttraumatic Stress Disorder: An Assessment of the Evidence* (Washington:

National Academies Press, 2008); and R. Bradley, et al., "A Multidimensional Meta-Analysis of Psychotherapy for PTSD," *American Journal of Psychiatry* 162, no. 2 (2005): 214–27.

39. J. Bisson, et al., "Psychological Treatments for Chronic Posttraumatic Stress Disorder: Systematic Review and Meta-Analysis," *British Journal of Psychiatry* 190 (2007): 97–104. See also L. H. Jaycox, E. B. Foa, and A. R. Morrall, "Influence of Emotional Engagement and Habituation on Exposure Therapy for PTSD," *Journal of Consulting and Clinical Psychology* 66 (1998): 185–92.

40. "Dropouts: in prolonged exposure (n = 53 [38%]); in present-centered therapy (n = 30 [21%]) (P = .002). The control group also had a high rate of casualties: 2 nonsuicidal deaths, 9 psychiatric hospitalizations, and 3 suicide attempts." P. P. Schnurr, et al., "Cognitive Behavioral Therapy for Posttraumatic Stress Disorder in Women," *JAMA* 297, no. 8 (2007): 820–30.

41. R. Bradley, et al., "A Multidimensional Meta-Analysis of Psychotherapy for PTSD," *American Journal of Psychiatry* 162, no. 2 (2005): 214–27.

42. J. H. Jaycox and E. B. Foa, "Obstacles in Implementing Exposure Therapy for PTSD: Case Discussions and Practical Solutions," *Clinical Psychology and Psychotherapy* 3, no. 3 (1996): 176–84. See also E. B. Foa, D. Hearst-Ikeda, and K. J. Perry, "Evaluation of a Brief Cognitive-Behavioral Program for the Prevention of Chronic PTSD in Recent Assault Victims," *Journal of Consulting and Clinical Psychology* 63 (1995): 948–55.

43. Alexander McFarlane personal communication.

44. R. K. Pitman, et al., "Psychiatric Complications During Flooding Therapy for Posttraumatic Stress Disorder," *Journal of Clinical Psychiatry* 52, no. 1 (January 1991): 17–20.

45. Jean Decety, Kalina J. Michalska, and Katherine D. Kinzler, "The Contribution of Emotion and Cognition to Moral Sensitivity: A Neurodevelopmental Study," Cerebral Cortex 22 no. 1 (2012): 209–20; Jean Decety, C. Daniel Batson, "Neuroscience Approaches to Interpersonal Sensitivity," 2, nos. 3-4 (2007).

46. K. H. Seal, et al., "VA Mental Health Services Utilization in Iraq and Afghanistan Veterans in the First Year of Receiving New Mental Health Diagnoses," *Journal of Traumatic Stress* 23 (2010): 5–16.

47. L. Jerome, "(+/-)-3,4-Methylenedioxymethamphetamine (MDMA, "Ecstasy") Investigator's Brochure," December 2007, available at www.maps.org/research/mdma/protocol/ib_mdma_new08.pdf (accessed August 16, 2012).

48. John H. Krystal, *et al.* "Chronic 3, 4-methylenedioxymethamphetamine (MDMA) use: effects on mood and neuropsychological function?." *The American Journal of Drug and Alcohol Abuse* 18.3 (1992): 331-341.

49. Mithoefer, Michael C., et al., "The safety and efficacy of±3, 4-methylenedioxymethamphetamine-assisted psychotherapy in subjects with chronic, treatment-resistant posttraumatic stress disorder: the first randomized controlled pilot study." *Journal of Psychopharmacology* 25.4 (2011): 439-452; M. C. Mithoefer, et al., "Durability of Improvement in Posttraumatic Stress Disorder Symptoms and Absence of Harmful Effects or Drug Dependency after 3, 4-Methylenedioxymethamphetamine-Assisted Psychotherapy: A Prospective Long-Term Follow-up Study," *Journal of Psychopharmacology* 27, no. 1 (2013): 28–39.

50. J. D. Bremner, "Neurobiology of Posttraumatic Stress Disorder," in *Posttraumatic Stress Disorder: A Critical Review,* ed. R. S. Rynoos (Lutherville, MD: Sidran Press, 1994), 43–64.

51. http://cdn.nextgov.com/nextgov/interstitial.html?v=2.1.1&rf=http%3A%2F%2Fwww.nextgov.com%2Fhealth%2F2011%2F01%2Fmilitarys-drug-policy-threatens-troops-health-doctors-say%2F48321%2F.

52. J. R. T. Davidson, "Drug Therapy of Posttraumatic Stress Disorder," *British Journal of Psychiatry* 160 (1992): 309–314. See also R. Famularo, R. Kinscherff, and T. Fenton, "Propranolol Treatment for Childhood Posttraumatic Stress Disorder Acute Type," *American Journal of Disorders of Childhood* 142 (1988): 1244–47; F. A. Fesler, "Valproate in Combat-Related Posttraumatic Stress Disorder," *Journal of Clinical Psychiatry* 52 (1991): 361–64; B. H. Herman, et al., "Naltrexone Decreases Self-Injurious Behavior," *Annals of Neurology* 22 (1987): 530–34; and B. A. van der Kolk, et al.,

"Fluoxetine in Posttraumatic Stress Disorder."

53. B. Van der Kolk, et al., "A Randomized Clinical Trial of EMDR, Fluoxetine and Pill Placebo in the Treatment of PTSD: Treatment Effects and Long-Term Maintenance," *Journal of Clinical Psychiatry* 68 (2007): 37–46.

54. R. A. Bryant, et al., "Treating Acute Stress Disorder: An Evaluation of Cognitive Behavior Therapy and Supportive Counseling Techniques," *American Journal of Psychiatry* 156, no. 11 (November 1999): 1780–86; N. P. Roberts et al., "Early Psychological Interventions to Treat Acute Traumatic Stress Symptoms," *Cochran Database of Systematic Reviews* 3 (March 2010).

55. This includes the alpha$_1$ receptor antagonist prazosin, the alpha$_2$ receptor antagonist clonidine, and the beta receptor antagonist propranolol. See M. J. Friedman and J. R. Davidson, "Pharmacotherapy for PTSD," in *Handbook of PTSD: Science and Practice*, ed. M. J. Friedman, T. M. Keane, and P. A. Resick (New York: Guilford Press, (2007), 376.

56. M. A. Raskind, et al., "A Parallel Group Placebo Controlled Study of Prazosin for Trauma Nightmares and Sleep Disturbance in Combat Veterans with Posttraumatic Stress Disorder," *Biological Psychiatry* 61, no. 8 (2007): 928–34. F. B. Taylor, et al., "Prazosin Effects on Objective Sleep Measures and Clinical Symptoms in Civilian Trauma Posttraumatic Stress Disorder: A Placebo-Controlled Study," *Biological Psychiatry* 63, no. 6 (2008): 629–32.

57. Lithium, lamotrigin, carbamazepine, divalproex, gabapentin, and topiramate may help to control trauma-related aggression and irritability. Valproate has been shown to be effective in several case reports with PTSD, including with military veteran patients with chronic PTSD. Friedman and Davidson, "Pharmacotherapy for PTSD"; F. A. Fesler, "Valproate in Combat-Related Posttraumatic Stress Disorder," *Journal of Clinical Psychiatry* 52, no. 9 (1991): 361–64. The following study showed a 37.4 percent reduction in PTSD S. Akuchekian and S. Amanat, "The Comparison of Topiramate and Placebo in the Treatment of Posttraumatic Stress Disorder: A Randomized, Double-Blind Study," *Journal of Research in Medical Sciences* 9, no. 5 (2004): 240–44.

58. G. Bartzokis, et al., "Adjunctive Risperidone in the Treatment of Chronic Combat-Related Posttraumatic Stress Disorder," *Biological Psychiatry* 57, no. 5 (2005): 474–79. See also D. B. Reich, et al., "A Preliminary Study of Risperidone in the Treatment of Posttraumatic Stress Disorder Related to Childhood Abuse in Women," *Journal of Clinical Psychiatry* 65, no. 12 (2004): 1601–1606.

59. The other methods include interventions that usually help traumatized individuals sleep, like the antidepressant trazodone, binaural beat apps, light/sound machines like Proteus (www.brainmachines.com), HRV monitors like hearthmath (http://www.heartmath.com/), and iRest, an effective yoga-based intervention. (http://www.irest.us/)

60. D. Wilson, "Child's Ordeal Shows Risks of Psychosis Drugs for Young," *New York Times*, September 1, 2010, available at http://www.nytimes.com/2010/09/02/business/02kids.html?pagewanted=all&_r=0.

61. M. Olfson, et al., "National Trends in the Office-Based Treatment of Children, Adolescents, and Adults with Antipsychotics," *Archives of General Psychiatry* 69, no. 12 (2012): 1247–56.

62. E. Harris, et al., "Perspectives on Systems of Care: Concurrent Mental Health Therapy Among Medicaid-Enrolled Youths Starting Antipsychotic Medications," *FOCUS* 10, no. 3 (2012): 401–407.

63. B. A. Van der Kolk, "The Body Keeps the Score: Memory and the Evolving Psychobiology of Posttraumatic Stress," *Harvard Review of Psychiatry* 1, no. 5 (1994): 253–65.

64. B. Brewin, "Mental Illness is the Leading Cause of Hospitalization for Active-Duty Troops," Nextgov.com, May 17, 2012, http://www.nextgov.com/health/2012/05/mental-illness-leading-cause-hospitalization-active-duty-troops/55797/.

65. Mental health drug expenditures, Department of Veterans affairs. http://www.veterans.senate.gov/imo/media/doc/For%20the%20Record%20-%20CCHR%204.30.14.pdf.

CHAPTER 14: LANGUAGE: MIRACLE AND TYRANNY

1. Dr. Spencer Eth to Bessel A. van der Kolk, March 2002.
2. J. Breuer and S. Freud, "The Physical Mechanisms of Hysterical Phenomena," in *The Standard Edition of the Complete Psychological Works of Sigmund Freud* (London: Hogarth Press, 1893). J. Breuer and S. Freud, *Studies on Hysteria* (New York: Basic Books, 2009).
3. T. E. Lawrence, *Seven Pillars of Wisdom* (New York: Doubleday, 1935).
4. E. B. Foa, et al., "The Posttraumatic Cognitions Inventory (PTCI): Development and Validation," *Psychological Assessment* 11, no. 3 (1999): 303–314.
5. K. Marlantes, *What It Is Like to Go to War* (New York: Grove Press, 2011).
6. Ibid., 114.
7. Ibid., 129.
8. H. Keller, *The World I Live In* (1908), ed. R. Shattuck (New York: NYRB Classics, 2004). See also R. Shattuck, "A World of Words," *New York Review of Books*, February 26, 2004.
9. H. Keller, *The Story of My Life*, ed. R. Shattuck and D. Herrmann (New York: Norton, 2003).
10. W. M. Kelley, et al., "Finding the Self? An Event-Related fMRI Study," *Journal of Cognitive Neuroscience* 14, no. 5 (2002): 785–94. See also N. A. Farb, et al., "Attending to the Present: Mindfulness Meditation Reveals Distinct Neural Modes of Self-Reference," *Social Cognitive and Affective Neuroscience* 2, no. 4 (2007): 313–22. P. M. Niedenthal, "Embodying Emotion," *Science* 316, no. 5827 (2007): 1002–1005; and J. M. Allman, "The Anterior Cingulate Cortex," *Annals of the New York Academy of Sciences* 935, no. 1 (2001): 107–117.
11. J. Kagan, dialogue with the Dalai Lama, Massachusetts Institute of Technology, 2006. http://www.mindandlife.org/about/history/.
12. A. Goldman and F. de Vignemont, "Is Social Cognition Embodied?" *Trends in Cognitive Sciences* 13, no. 4 (2009): 154–59. See also A. D. Craig, "How Do You Feel—Now? The Anterior Insula and Human Awareness," Nature Reviews Neuroscience 10 (2009): 59–70; H. D. Critchley, "Neural Mechanisms of Autonomic, Affective, and Cognitive Integration," *Journal of Comparative Neurology* 493, no. 1 (2005): 154–66; T. D. Wager, et al., "Prefrontal-Subcortical Pathways Mediating Successful Emotion Regulation," *Neuron* 59, no. 6 (2008): 1037–50; K. N. Ochsner, et al., "Rethinking Feelings: An fMRI Study of the Cognitive Regulation of Emotion," *Journal of Cognitive Neuroscience* 14, no. 8 (2002): 1215–29; A. D'Argembeau, et al., "Self-Reflection Across Time: Cortical Midline Structures Differentiate Between Present and Past Selves," *Social Cognitive and Affective Neuroscience* 3, no. 3 (2008): 244–52; Y. Ma, et al., "Sociocultural Patterning of Neural Activity During Self-Reflection," *Social Cognitive and Affective Neuroscience* 9, no. 1 (2014): 73–80; R. N. Spreng, R. A. Mar, and A. S. Kim, "The Common Neural Basis of Autobiographical Memory, Prospection, Navigation, Theory of Mind, and the Default Mode: A Quantitative Meta-Analysis," *Journal of Cognitive Neuroscience* 21, no. 3 (2009): 489–510; H. D. Critchley, "The Human Cortex Responds to an Interoceptive Challenge," *Proceedings of the National Academy of Sciences of the United States of America* 101, no. 17 (2004): 6333–34; and C. Lamm, C. D. Batson, and J. Decety, "The Neural Substrate of Human Empathy: Effects of Perspective-Taking and Cognitive Appraisal," *Journal of Cognitive Neuroscience* 19, no. 1 (2007): 42–58.
13. J. W. Pennebaker, *Opening Up: The Healing Power of Expressing Emotions* (New York: Guilford Press, 2012), 12.
14. Ibid., p. 19.

15. Ibid., p.35.

16. Ibid., p. 50.

17. J. W. Pennebaker, J. K. Kiecolt-Glaser, and R. Glaser, "Disclosure of Traumas and Immune Function: Health Implications for Psychotherapy," *Journal of Consulting and Clinical Psychology* 56, no. 2 (1988): 239–45.

18. D. A. Harris, "Dance/Movement Therapy Approaches to Fostering Resilience and Recovery Among African Adolescent Torture Survivors," *Torture* 17, no. 2 (2007): 134–55; M. Bensimon, D. Amir, and Y. Wolf, "Drumming Through Trauma: Music Therapy with Posttraumatic Soldiers," *Arts in Psychotherapy* 35, no. 1 (2008): 34–48; M. Weltman, "Movement Therapy with Children Who Have Been Sexually Abused," *American Journal of Dance Therapy* 9, no. 1 (1986): 47–66; H. Englund, "Death, Trauma and Ritual: Mozambican Refugees in Malawi," *Social Science & Medicine* 46, no. 9 (1998): 1165–74; H. Tefferi, Building on Traditional Strengths: The Unaccompanied Refugee Children from South Sudan (1996); D. Tolfree, *Restoring Playfulness: Different Approaches to Assisting Children Who Are Psychologically Affected by War or Displacement* (Stockholm: Rädda Barnen, 1996), 158–73; N. Boothby, "Mobilizing Communities to Meet the Psychosocial Needs of Children in War and Refugee Crises," in *Minefields in Their Hearts: The Mental Health of Children in War and Communal Violence*, ed. R. Apfel and B. Simon (New Haven, Yale Universit Press, 1996), 149–64; S. Sandel, S. Chaiklin, and A. Lohn, *Foundations of Dance/Movement Therapy: The Life and Work of Marian Chace* (Columbia, MD: American Dance Therapy Association, 1993); K. Callaghan, "Movement Psychotherapy with Adult Survivors of Political Torture and Organized Violence," *Arts in Psychotherapy* 20, no. 5 (1993): 411–21; A. E. L. Gray, "The Body Remembers: Dance Movement Therapy with an Adult Survivor of Torture," *American Journal of Dance Therapy* 23, no. 1 (2001): 29–43.

19. A. M. Krantz, and J. W. Pennebaker, "Expressive Dance, Writing, Trauma, and Health: When Words Have a Body." *Whole Person Healthcare* 3 (2007): 201–29.

20. P. Fussell, *The Great War and Modern Memory* (London: Oxford University Press, 1975).

21. Theses findings have been replicated in the following studies: J. D. Bremner, "Does Stress Damage the Brain?" *Biological Psychiatry* 45, no. 7 (1999): 797–805; I. Liberzon, et al., "Brain Activation in PTSD in Response to Trauma-Related Stimuli," *Biological Psychiatry* 45, no. 7 (1999): 817–26; L. M. Shin, et al., "Visual Imagery and Perception in Posttraumatic Stress Disorder: A Positron Emission Tomographic Investigation," *Archives of General Psychiatry* 54, no. 3 (1997): 233–41; L. M. Shin, et al., "Regional Cerebral Blood Flow During Script-Driven Imagery in Childhood Sexual Abuse–Related PTSD: A PET Investigation," *American Journal of Psychiatry* 156, no. 4 (1999): 575–84.

22. I am not sure if this term originated with me or with Peter Levine. I own a video where he credits me, but most of what I have learned about pendulation I've learned from him.

23. A small body of evidence offers support for claims that exposure/acupoints stimulation yields stronger outcomes and exposures strategies that incorporate conventional relaxation techniques. (www.vetcases.com). D. Church, et al., "Single-Session Reduction of the Intensity of Traumatic Memories in Abused Adolescents After EFT: A Randomized Controlled Pilot Study," *Traumatology* 18, no. 3 (2012): 73–79; and D. Feinstein and D. Church, "Modulating Gene Expression Through Psychotherapy: The Contribution of Noninvasive Somatic Interventions," *Review of General Psychology* 14, no. 4 (2010): 283–95.

24. T. Gil, et al., "Cognitive Functioning in Posttraumatic Stress Disorder," *Journal of Traumatic Stress* 3, no. 1 (1990): 29–45; J. J. Vasterling, et al., "Attention, Learning, and Memory Performances and Intellectual Resources in Vietnam Veterans: PTSD and No Disorder Comparisons," *Neuropsychology* 16, no. 1 (2002): 5.

25. In a neuroimaging study the PTSD subjects deactivated the speech area of their brain, Broca's area, in response to neutral words. In other words: the decreased Broca's area functioning that we had found in PTSD patients (see chapter 3) did not only occur in response to traumatic memories; it also happened when they were asked to pay attention to neutral words. This means that, as a group, traumatized

patients have a harder time to articulate what they feel and think about ordinary events. The PTSD group also had decreased activation of the medial prefrontal cortex (mPFC), the frontal lobe area that, as we have seen, conveys awareness of one's self, and dampens activation of the amygdala, the smoke detector. This made it harder for them to suppress the brain's fear response in response to a simple language task and again, made it harder to pay attention and go on with their lives. See: Moores, K. A., Clark, C. R., McFarlane, A. C., Brown, G. C., Puce, A., & Taylor, D. J. (2008). Abnormal recruitment of working memory updating networks during maintenance of trauma-neutral information in posttraumatic stress disorder. Psychiatry Research: Neuroimaging, 163(2), 156–170.

26. J. Breuer and S. Freud, "The Physical Mechanisms of Hysterical Phenomena," in *The Standard Edition of the Complete Psychological Works of Sigmund Freud* (London: Hogarth Press, 1893).

27. D. L. Schacter, *Searching for Memory* (New York: Basic Books, 1996).

CHAPTER 15: LETTING GO OF THE PAST: EMDR

1. F. Shapiro, *EMDR: The Breakthrough Eye Movement Therapy for Overcoming Anxiety, Stress, and Trauma* (New York: Basic Books, 2004).

2. B. A. van der Kolk, et al., "A Randomized Clinical Trial of Eye Movement Desensitization and Reprocessing (EMDR), Fluoxetine, and Pill Placebo in the Treatment of Posttraumatic Stress Disorder: Treatment Effects and Long-Term Maintenance," *Journal of Clinical Psychiatry 68*, no. 1 (2007): 37–46.

3. J. G. Carlson, et al., "Eye Movement Desensitization and Reprocessing (EDMR) Treatment for Combat-Related Posttraumatic Stress Disorder," *Journal of Traumatic Stress* 11, no. 1 (1998): 3–24.

4. J. D. Payne, et al., "Sleep Increases False Recall of Semantically Related Words in the Deese-Roediger-McDermott Memory Task," *Sleep* 29 (2006): A373.

5. B. A. van der Kolk and C. P. Ducey, "The Psychological Processing of Traumatic Experience: Rorschach Patterns in PTSD," *Journal of Traumatic Stress* 2, no. 3 (1989): 259–74.

6. M. Jouvet, *The Paradox of Sleep: The Story of Dreaming*, trans. Laurence Garey (Cambridge, MA: MIT Press, 1999).

7. R. Greenwald, "Eye Movement Desensitization and Reprocessing (EMDR): A New Kind of Dreamwork?" *Dreaming* 5, no. 1 (1995): 51–55.

8. R. Cartwright, et al., "REM Sleep Reduction, Mood Regulation and Remission in Untreated Depression," *Psychiatry Research* 121, no. 2 (2003): 159–67. See also R. Cartwright, et al., "Role of REM Sleep and Dream Affect in Overnight Mood Regulation: A Study of Normal Volunteers," *Psychiatry Research* 81, no. 1 (1998): 1–8.

9. R. Greenberg, C. A. Pearlman, and D. Gampel, "War Neuroses and the Adaptive Function of REM Sleep," *British Journal of Medical Psychology* 45, no. 1 1972): 27–33. Ramon Greenberg and Chester Pearlman, as well as our lab, found that traumatized veterans wake themselves up as soon as they enter a REM period. While many traumatized individuals use alcohol to help them sleep, they thereby keep themselves from the full benefits of dreaming (the integration and transformation of memory) and thereby may contribute to preventing the resolution of their PTSD.

10. B. van der Kolk, et al., "Nightmares and Trauma: A Comparison of Nightmares After Combat with Lifelong Nightmares in Veterans," *American Journal of Psychiatry* 141, no. 2 (1984): 187–90.

11. N. Breslau, et al., "Sleep Disturbance and Psychiatric Disorders: A Longitudinal Epidemiological Study of Young Adults," *Biological Psychiatry* 39, no. 6 (1996): 411–18.

12. R. Stickgold, et al., "Sleep-Induced Changes in Associative Memory," *Journal of Cognitive Neuroscience* 11, no. 2 (1999): 182–93. See also R. Stickgold, "Of Sleep, Memories and Trauma," *Nature Neuroscience* 10, no. 5 (2007): 540–42; and B. Rasch, et al., "Odor Cues During Slow-Wave Sleep Prompt Declarative Memory Consolidation," *Science* 315, no. 5817 (2007): 1426–29.

13. E. J. Wamsley, et al., "Dreaming of a Learning Task Is Associated with Enhanced Sleep-Dependent Memory Consolidation," *Current Biology* 20, no. 9, (May 11, 2010): 850–55.

14. R. Stickgold, "Sleep-Dependent Memory Consolidation," *Nature* 437 (2005): 1272–78.

15. R. Stickgold, et al., "Sleep-Induced Changes in Associative Memory," *Journal of Cognitive Neuroscience* 11, no. 2 (1999): 182–93.

16. J. Williams, et al., "Bizarreness in Dreams and Fantasies: Implications for the Activation-Synthesis Hypothesis," *Consciousness and Cognition* 1, no. 2 (1992): 172–85. See also Stickgold, et al., "Sleep-Induced Changes in Associative Memory."

17. M. P. Walker, et al., "Cognitive Flexibility Across the Sleep-Wake Cycle: REM-Sleep Enhancement of Anagram Problem Solving," *Cognitive Brain Research* 14 (2002): 317–24.

18. R. Stickgold, "EMDR: A Putative Neurobiological Mechanism of Action," *Journal of Clinical Psychology* 58 (2002): 61–75.

19. There are several studies on how eye movements help to process and transform traumatic memories. M. Sack, et al., "Alterations in Autonomic Tone During Trauma Exposure Using Eye Movement Desensitization and Reprocessing (EMDR)—Results of a Preliminary Investigation," *Journal of Anxiety Disorders* 22, no. 7 (2008): 1264–71; B. Letizia, F. Andrea, and C. Paolo, Neuroanatomical Changes After Eye Movement Desensitization and Reprocessing (EMDR) Treatment in Posttraumatic Stress Disorder, *The Journal of Neuropsychiatry and Clinical Neurosciences*, 19, no. 4 (2007): 475–76; P. Levin, S. Lazrove, and B. van der Kolk, (1999). What Psychological Testing and Neuroimaging Tell Us About the Treatment of Posttraumatic Stress Disorder by Eye Movement Desensitization and Reprocessing, *Journal of Anxiety Disorders*, 13, nos. 1–2, 159–72; M. L. Harper, T. Rasolkhani Kalhorn, J. F. Drozd, "On the Neural Basis of EMDR Therapy: Insights from Qeeg Studies, *Traumatology*, 15, no. 2 (2009): 81–95; K. Lansing, D. G. Amen, C. Hanks, L. Rudy, "High-Resolution Brain SPECT Imaging and Eye Movement Desensitization and Reprocessing in Police Officers with PTSD," *The Journal of Neuropsychiatry and Clinical Neurosciences* 17, no. 4 (2005): 526–32; T. Ohtani, K. Matsuo, K. Kasai, T. Kato, and N. Kato, "Hemodynamic Responses of Eye Movement Desensitization and Reprocessing in Posttraumatic Stress Disorder. *Neuroscience Research*, 65, no. 4 (2009): 375–83; M. Pagani, G. Högberg, D. Salmaso, D. Nardo, Ö. Sundin, C. Jonsson, and T. Hällström, "Effects of EMDR Psychotherapy on ^{99m}tc-HMPAO Distribution in Occupation-Related PostTraumatic Stress Disorder," *Nuclear Medicine Communications* 28 (2007): 757–65; H. P. Söndergaard and U. Elofsson, "Psychophysiological Studies of EMDR," *Journal of EMDR Practice and Research* 2, no. 4 (2008): 282–88.

CHAPTER 16: LEARNING TO INHABIT YOUR BODY: YOGA

1. Acupuncture and acupressure are widely practiced among trauma-oriented clinicians and is beginning to be systematically studied as a treatment for clinical PTSD. M. Hollifield, et al., "Acupuncture for Posttraumatic Stress Disorder: A Randomized Controlled Pilot Trial," *Journal of Nervous and Mental Disease* 195, no. 6 (2007): 504–513. Studies that use fMRI to measure the effects of acupuncture on the areas of the brain associated with fear report acupuncture to produce rapid regulation of these brain regions. K. K. Hui, et al., "The Integrated Response of the Human Cerebro-Cerebellar and Limbic Systems to Acupuncture Stimulation at ST 36 as Evidenced by fMRI," *NeuroImage* 27 (2005): 479–96; J. Fang, et al., "The Salient Characteristics of the Central Effects of Acupuncture Needling: Limbic-Paralimbic-Neocortical Network Modulation," *Human Brain Mapping* 30 (2009): 1196–206. D. Feinstein, "Rapid Treatment of PTSD: Why Psychological Exposure with Acupoint Tapping May Be Effective," *Psychotherapy: Theory, Research, Practice, Training* 47, no. 3 (2010): 385–402; D. Church, et al., "Psychological Trauma Symptom Improvement in Veterans Using EFT (Emotional Freedom Technique): A Randomized Controlled Trial," *Journal of Nervous and Mental Disease* 201 (2013): 153–60; D. Church, G. Yount, and A. J. Brooks, "The Effect of Emotional Freedom Techniques (EFT) on Stress Biochemistry: A Randomized Controlled Trial," *Journal of Nervous and Mental Disease* 200 (2012): 891–96; R. P. Dhond, N. Kettner, and V. Napadow, "Neuroimaging Acupuncture Effects in the Human Brain," *Journal of Alternative and Complementary Medicine* 13

(2007): 603–616; K. K. Hui, et al., "Acupuncture Modulates the Limbic System and Subcortical Gray Structures of the Human Brain: Evidence from fMRI Studies in Normal Subjects," *Human Brain Mapping* 9 (2000): 13–25.

2. M. Sack, J. W. Hopper, and F. Lamprecht, "Low Respiratory Sinus Arrhythmia and Prolonged Psychophysiological Arousal in Posttraumatic Stress Disorder: Heart Rate Dynamics and Individual Differences in Arousal Regulation," *Biological Psychiatry* 55, no. 3 (2004): 284–90. See also H. Cohen, et al., "Analysis of Heart Rate Variability in Posttraumatic Stress Disorder Patients in Response to a Trauma-Related Reminder," *Biological Psychiatry* 44, no. 10 (1998): 1054–59; H. Cohen, et al., "Long-Lasting Behavioral Effects of Juvenile Trauma in an Animal Model of PTSD Associated with a Failure of the Autonomic Nervous System to Recover," *European Neuropsychopharmacology* 17, no. 6 (2007): 464–77; and H. Wahbeh and B. S. Oken, "Peak High-Frequency HRV and Peak Alpha Frequency Higher in PTSD," *Applied Psychophysiology and Biofeedback* 38, no. 1 (2013): 57–69.

3. J. W. Hopper, et al., "Preliminary Evidence of Parasympathetic Influence on Basal Heart Rate in Posttraumatic Stress Disorder," *Journal of Psychosomatic Research* 60, no. 1 (2006): 83–90.

4. Arieh Shalev at Hadassah Medical School in Jerusalem and Roger Pitman's experiments at Harvard also pointed in this direction: A. Y. Shalev, et al., "Auditory Startle Response in Trauma Survivors with Posttraumatic Stress Disorder: A Prospective Study," *American Journal of Psychiatry* 157, no. 2 (2000): 255–61; R. K. Pitman, et al., "Psychophysiologic Assessment of Posttraumatic Stress Disorder Imagery in Vietnam Combat Veterans," *Archives of General Psychiatry* 44, no. 11 (1987): 970–75; A. Y. Shalev, et al., "A Prospective Study of Heart Rate Response Following Trauma and the Subsequent Development of Posttraumatic Stress Disorder," *Archives of General Psychiatry* 55, no. 6 (1998): 553–59.

5. P. Lehrer, Y. Sasaki, and Y. Saito, "Zazen and Cardiac Variability," *Psychosomatic Medicine* 61, no. 6 (1999): 812–21. See also R. Sovik, "The Science of Breathing: The Yogic View," *Progress in Brain Research* 122 (1999): 491–505; P. Philippot, G. Chapelle, and S. Blairy, "Respiratory Feedback in the Generation of Emotion," *Cognition & Emotion* 16, no. 5 (2002): 605–627; A. Michalsen, et al., "Rapid Stress Reduction and Anxiolysis Among Distressed Women as a Consequence of a Three-Month Intensive Yoga Program," *Medcal Science Monitor* 11, no. 12 (2005): 555–61; G. Kirkwood et al., "Yoga for Anxiety: A Systematic Review of the Research Evidence," *British Journal of Sports Medicine* 39 (2005): 884–91; K. Pilkington, et al., "Yoga for Depression: The Research Evidence," *Journal of Affective Disorders* 89 (2005): 13–24; and P. Gerbarg and R. Brown, "Yoga: A Breath of Relief for Hurricane Katrina Refugees," *Current Psychiatry* 4 (2005): 55–67.

6. B. Cuthbert et al., "Strategies of Arousal Control: Biofeedback, Meditation, and Motivation," *Journal of Experimental Psychology* 110 (1981): 518–46. See also S. B. S. Khalsa, "Yoga as a Therapeutic Intervention: A Bibliometric Analysis of Published Research Studies," *Indian Journal of Physiology and Pharmacology* 48 (2004): 269–85; M. M. Delmonte, "Meditation as a Clinical Intervention Strategy: A Brief Review," *International Journal of Psychosomatics* 33 (1986): 9–12; I. Becker, "Uses of Yoga in Psychiatry and Medicine," in *Complementary and Alternative Medicine and Psychiatry*, vol. 19, ed. P. R. Muskin PR (Washington: American Psychiatric Press, 2008); L. Bernardi, et al., "Slow Breathing Reduces Chemoreflex Response to Hypoxia and Hypercapnia, and Increases Baroreflex Sensitivity," *Journal of Hypertension* 19, no. 12 (2001): 2221–29; R. P. Brown and P. L. Gerbarg, "Sudarshan Kriya Yogic Breathing in the Treatment of Stress, Anxiety, and Depression: Part I: Neurophysiologic Model," *Journal of Alternative and Complementary Medicine* 11 (2005): 189–201; R. P. Brown and P. L. Gerbarg, "Sudarshan Kriya Yogic Breathing in the Treatment of Stress, Anxiety, and Depression: Part II: Clinical Applications and Guidelines," *Journal of Alternative and Complementary Medicine* 11 (2005): 711–17; C. C. Streeter, et al., "Yoga Asana Sessions Increase Brain GABA Levels: A Pilot Study," *Journal of Alternative and Complementary Medicine* 13 (2007): 419–26; and C. C. Streeter, et al., "Effects of Yoga Versus Walking on Mood, Anxiety, and Brain GABA Levels: A Randomized Controlled MRS Study," *Journal of Alternative and Complementary Medicine* 16 (2010): 1145–52.

7. There are dozens of scientific articles showing the positive effect of yoga for various medical conditions. The following is a small sample: S. B. Khalsa, "Yoga as a Therapeutic Intervention"; P. Grossman, et al., "Mindfulness-Based Stress Reduction and Health Benefits: A Meta-Analysis," *Journal of Psychosomatic Research* 57 (2004): 35–43; K. Sherman, et al., "Comparing Yoga, Exercise, and a Self-Care Book for Chronic Low Back Pain: A Randomized, Controlled Trial," *Annals of Internal Medicine* 143 (2005): 849–56; K. A. Williams, et al., "Effect of Iyengar Yoga Therapy for Chronic Low Back Pain," *Pain* 115 (2005): 107–117; R. B. Saper, et al., "Yoga for Chronic Low Back Pain in a Predominantly Minority Population: A Pilot Randomized Controlled Trial," *Alternative Therapies in Health and Medicine* 15 (2009): 18–27; J. W. Carson, et al., "Yoga for Women with Metastatic Breast Cancer: Results from a Pilot Study," *Journal of Pain and Symptom Management* 33 (2007): 331–41.

8. B. A. van der Kolk, et al., "Yoga as an Adjunctive Therapy for PTSD," *Journal of Clinical Psychiatry* 75, no. 6 (June 2014): 559–65.

9. A California company, HeartMath, has developed nifty devices and computer games that are both fun and effective in helping people to achieve better HRV. To date nobody has studied whether simple devices such as those developed by HeartMath can reduce PTSD symptoms, but this very likely the case. (see in www.heartmath.org.)

10. As of this writing there are twenty-four apps available on iTunes that claim to be able to help increase HRV, such as emWave, HeartMath, and GPS4Soul.

11. B. A. van der Kolk, "Clinical Implications of Neuroscience Research in PTSD," *Annals of the New York Academy of Sciences* 1071, no. 1 (2006): 277–93.

12. S. Telles, et al., "Alterations of Auditory Middle Latency Evoked Potentials During Yogic Consciously Regulated Breathing and Attentive State of Mind," *International Journal of Psychophysiology* 14, no. 3 (1993): 189–98. See also P. L. Gerbarg, "Yoga and Neuro-Psychoanalysis," in *Bodies in Treatment: The Unspoken Dimension*, ed. Frances Sommer Anderson (New York, Analytic Press, 2008), 127–50.

13. D. Emerson and E. Hopper, *Overcoming Trauma Through Yoga: Reclaiming Your Body* (Berkeley, North Atlantic Books, 2011).

14. A. Damasio, *The Feeling of What Happens: Body and Emotion in the Making of Consciousness* (New York, Hartcourt, 1999).

15. "Interoception" is the scientific name for this basic self-sensing ability. Brain-imaging studies of traumatized people have repeatedly shown problems in the areas of the brain related to physical self-awareness, particularly an area called the insula. J. W. Hopper, et al., "Neural Correlates of Reexperiencing, Avoidance, and Dissociation in PTSD: Symptom Dimensions and Emotion Dysregulation in Responses to Script-Driven Trauma Imagery," *Journal of Traumatic Stress* 20, no. 5 (2007): 713–25. See also I. A. Strigo, et al., "Neural Correlates of Altered Pain Response in Women with Posttraumatic Stress Disorder from Intimate Partner Violence," *Biological Psychiatry* 68, no. 5 (2010): 442–50; G. A. Fonzo, et al., "Exaggerated and Disconnected Insular-Amygdalar Blood Oxygenation Level-Dependent Response to Threat-Related Emotional Faces in Women with Intimate-Partner Violence Posttraumatic Stress Disorder," *Biological Psychiatry* 68, no. 5 (2010): 433–41; P. A. Frewen, et al., "Social Emotions and Emotional Valence During Imagery in Women with PTSD: Affective and Neural Correlates," *Psychological Trauma: Theory, Research, Practice, and Policy* 2, no. 2 (2010): 145–57; K. Felmingham, et al., "Dissociative Responses to Conscious and Non-conscious Fear Impact Underlying Brain Function in Posttraumatic Stress Disorder," *Psychological Medicine* 38, no. 12 (2008): 1771–80; A. N. Simmons, et al., "Functional Activation and Neural Networks in Women with Posttraumatic Stress Disorder Related to Intimate Partner Violence," *Biological Psychiatry* 64, no. 8 (2008): 681–90; R. J. L. Lindauer, et al., "Effects of Psychotherapy on Regional Cerebral Blood Flow During Trauma Imagery in Patients with Posttraumatic Stress Disorder: A Randomized Clinical Trial," *Psychological Medicine* 38, no. 4 (2008): 543–54 and A. Etkin and T. D. Wager, "Functional Neuroimaging of Anxiety: A Meta-Analysis of Emotional Processing in PTSD,

Social Anxiety Disorder, and Specific Phobia," *American Journal of Psychiatry* 164, no. 10 (2007): 1476–88.

16. J. C. Nemiah and P. E. Sifneos, "Psychosomatic Illness: A Problem in Communication," *Psychotherapy and Psychosomatics* 18, no. 1–6 (1970): 154–60. See also G. J. Taylor, R. M. Bagby, and J. D. A. Parker, *Disorders of Affect Regulation: Alexithymia in Medical and Psychiatric Illness* (Cambridge: Cambridge University Press, 1997).

17. A. R. Damásio, *The Feeling of What Happens: Body and Emotion and the Making of Consciousness* (Random House, 2000), 28.

18. B. A. van der Kolk, "Clinical Implications of Neuroscience Research in PTSD," *Annals of the New York Academy of Sciences* 1071, no. 1 (2006): 277–93. See also B. K. Hölzel, et al., "How Does Mindfulness Meditation Work? Proposing Mechanisms of Action from a Conceptual and Neural Perspective," *Perspectives on Psychological Science* 6, no. 6 (2011): 537–59.

19. B. K. Hölzel, et al., "Mindfulness Practice Leads to Increases in Regional Brain Gray Matter Density," *Psychiatry Research: Neuroimaging* 191, no. 1 (2011): 36–43. See also B. K. Hölzel, et al., "Stress Reduction Correlates with Structural Changes in the Amygdala," *Social Cognitive and Affective Neuroscience* 5, no. 1 (2010): 11–17; and S. W. Lazar, et al., "Meditation Experience Is Associated with Increased Cortical Thickness," *NeuroReport* 16 (2005): 1893–97.

CHAPTER 17: PUTTING THE PIECES TOGETHER: SELF-LEADERSHIP

1. R. A. Goulding and R. C. Schwartz, *The Mosaic Mind: Empowering the Tormented Selves of Child Abuse Survivors* (New York: Norton, 1995), 4.

2. J. G. Watkins and H. H. Watkins, *Ego States* (New York: Norton, 1997). Jung calls personality parts archetypes and complexes; cognitive psychology schemes and the DID literature refers to them as alters. See also J. G. Watkins and H. H. Watkins, "Theory and Practice of Ego State Therapy: A Short-Term Therapeutic Approach," *Short-Term Approaches to Psychotherapy* 3 (1979): 176–220; J. G. Watkins and H. H. Watkins, "Ego States and Hidden Observers," *Journal of Altered States of Consciousness* 5, no. 1 (1979): 3–18; and C. G. Jung, *Lectures: Psychology and Religion* (New Haven CT: Yale University Press, 1960).

3. W. James, *The Principles of Psychology* (New York: Holt, 1890), 206.

4. C. Jung, *Collected Works*, vol. 9, *The Archetypes and the Collective Unconscious* (Princeton, NJ: Princeton University Press, 1955/1968), 330.

5. C. Jung, *Collected Works*, vol. 10, *Civilization in Transition* (Princeton, NJ: Princeton University Press, 1957/1964), 540.

6. Ibid., 133.

7. M. S. Gazzaniga, *The Social Brain: Discovering the Networks of the Mind* (New York: Basic Books, 1985), 90.

8. Ibid., 356.

9. M, Minsky, *The Society of Mind* (New York: Simon & Schuster, 1988), 51.

10. Goulding and Schwartz, *Mosaic Mind*, p. 290.

11. O. van der Hart, E. R. Nijenhuis, and K. Steele, *The Haunted Self: Structural Dissociation and the Treatment of Chronic Traumatization* (New York: WW Norton, 2006); R. P. Kluft, *Shelter from the Storm* (self-published, 2013).

12. R. Schwartz, *Internal Family Systems Therapy* (New York: Guilford Press, 1995).

13. Ibid., p. 34.

14. Ibid., p. 19.

15. Goulding and Schwartz, *Mosaic Mind*, 63.

16. J. G. Watkins, 1997, illustrates this as an example of personifying depression: "We need to know what the imaginal sense of the depression is and who, which character, suffers it."

17. Richard Schwartz, personal communication.

18. Goulding and Schwartz, *Mosaic Mind*, 33.

19. A. W. Evers, et al., "Tailored Cognitive-Behavioral Therapy in Early Rheumatoid Arthritis for Patients at Risk: A Randomized Controlled Trial," *Pain* 100, no. 1–2 (2002): 141–53; E. K. Pradhan, et al., "Effect of Mindfulness-Based Stress Reduction in Rheumatoid Arthritis Patients," *Arthritis & Rheumatology* 57, no. 7 (2007): p. 1134–42; J. M. Smyth, et al., "Effects of Writing About Stressful Experiences on Symptom Reduction in Patients with Asthma or Rheumatoid Arthritis: A Randomized Trial," *JAMA* 281, no. 14 (1999): 1304–9; L. Sharpe, et al., "Long-Term Efficacy of a Cognitive Behavioural Treatment from a Randomized Controlled Trial for Patients Recently Diagnosed with Rheumatoid Arthritis," *Rheumatology (Oxford)* 42, no. 3 (2003): 435–41; H. A. Zangi, et al., "A Mindfulness-Based Group Intervention to Reduce Psychological Distress and Fatigue in Patients with Inflammatory Rheumatic Joint Diseases: A Randomised Controlled Trial," *Annals of the Rheumatic Diseases* 71, no. 6 (2012): 911–17.

CHAPTER 18: FILLING IN THE HOLES: CREATING STRUCTURES

1. Pesso Boyden System Psychomotor. See http://pbsp.com/.

2. D. Goleman, *Social Intelligence: The New Science of Human Relationships* (Random House Digital, 2006).

3. A. Pesso, "PBSP: Pesso Boyden System Psychomotor," in *Getting in Touch: A Guide to Body-Centered Therapies*, ed. S. Caldwell (Wheaton, IL: Theosophical Publishing House, 1997); A. Pesso, *Movement in Psychotherapy: Psychomotor Techniques and Training* (New York: New York University Press, 1969); A. Pesso, *Experience in Action: A Psychomotor Psychology* (New York: New York University Press, 1973); A. Pesso and J. Crandell, eds., *Moving Psychotherapy: Theory and Application of Pesso System/Psychomotor* (Cambridge, MA: Brookline Books, 1991); M. Scarf, *Secrets, Lies, and Betrayals* (New York: Ballantine Books, 2005); M. van Attekum, *Aan Den Lijve* (Netherlands: Pearson Assessment, 2009); and A. Pesso, "The Externalized Realization of the Unconscious and the Corrective Experience," in *Handbook of Body-Psychotherapy / Handbuch der Körperpsychotherapie*, ed. H. Weiss and G. Marlock (Stuttgart,Germany: Schattauer, 2006).

4. Luiz Pessoa, and Ralph Adolphs, "Emotion Processing and the Amygdala: from a 'Low Road' to 'Many Roads' of Evaluating Biological Significance." *Nature Reviews Neuroscience* 11, no. 11 (2010): 773–83.

CHAPTER 19: REWIRING THE BRAIN: NEUROFEEDBACK

1. H. H. Jasper, P. Solomon, and C. Bradley, "Electroencephalographic Analyses of Behavior Problem Children," *American Journal of Psychiatry* 95 (1938): 641–58; P. Solomon, H. H. Jasper, and C. Braley, "Studies in Behavior Problem Children," *American Neurology and Psychiatry* 38 (1937): 1350–51.

2. Martin Teicher at Harvard Medical School, has done extensive research that documents temporal lobe abnormalities in adults who were abused as children: M. H. Teicher et al., "The Neurobiological Consequences of Early Stress and Childhood Maltreatment," *Neuroscience & Biobehavioral Reviews* 27, no. 1–2) (2003): 33–44; M. H. Teicher et al., "Early Childhood Abuse and Limbic System Ratings in Adult Psychiatric Outpatients," *Journal of Neuropsychiatry & Clinical Neurosciences* 5, no. 3 (1993): 301–6; M. H. Teicher, et al., "Sticks, Stones and Hurtful Words: Combined Effects of Childhood Maltreatment Matter Most," *American Journal of Psychiatry* (2012).

3. Sebern F. Fisher, *Neurofeedback in the Treatment of Developmental Trauma: Calming the Fear-Driven Brain.* (New York: Norton, 2014).

4. J. N. Demos, *Getting Started with Neurofeedback* (New York: WW Norton, 2005). See also R. J. Davidson, "Affective Style and Affective Disorders: Prospectives from Affective Neuroscience," *Cognition and Emotion* 12, no. 3 (1998): 307–30; and R. J. Davidson, et al., "Regional Brain Function, Emotion and Disorders of Emotion," *Current Opinion in Neurobiology* 9 (1999): 228–34.

5. J. Kamiya, "Conscious Control of Brain Waves," *Psychology Today*, April 1968, 56–60. See also D. P. Nowlis, and J. Kamiya, "The Control of Electroencephalographic Alpha Rhythms Through Auditory Feedback and the Associated Mental Activity," *Psychophysiology* 6, no. 4 (1970): 476–84 and D. Lantz and M. B. Sterman, "Neuropsychological Assessment of Subjects with Uncontrolled Epilepsy: Effects of EEG Feedback Training," *Epilepsia* 29, no. 2 (1988): 163–71.

6. M. B. Sterman, L. R. Macdonald, and R. K. Stone, "Biofeedback Training of the Sensorimotor Electroencephalogram Rhythm in Man: Effects on Epilepsy," *Epilepsia* 15, no. 3 (1974): 395–416. A recent meta-analysis of eighty-seven studies showed that neurofeedback led to a significant reduction in seizure frequency in approximately 80 percent of epileptics who received the training. Gabriel Tan, et al., "Meta-Analysis of EEG Biofeedback in Treating Epilepsy," *Clinical EEG and Neuroscience* 40, no. 3 (2009): 173–79.

7. This is part of the same circuit of self-awareness that I described in chapter 5. Alvaro Pascual-Leone has shown how, when one temporarily knocks out the area above the medial prefrontal cortex with transcranial magnetic stimulation (TMS), people can temporarily not identify whom they are looking at when they stare into the mirror. J. Pascual-Leone, "Mental Attention, Consciousness, and the Progressive Emergence of Wisdom," *Journal of Adult Development* 7, no. 4 (2000): 241–54.

8. http://www.eegspectrum.com/intro-to-neurofeedback/.

9. S. Rauch, et al., "Symptom Provocation Study Using Positron Emission Tomography and Script Driven Imagery," *Archives of General Psychiatry* 53 (1996): 380–87. Three other studies using a new way of imaging the brain, magnetoencephalography (MEG), showed that people with PTSD suffer from increased activation of the right temporal cortex: C. Catani, et al., "Pattern of Cortical Activation During Processing of Aversive Stimuli in Traumatized Survivors of War and Torture," *European Archives of Psychiatry and Clinical Neuroscience* 259, no. 6 (2009): 340–51; B. E. Engdahl, et al., "Posttraumatic Stress Disorder: A Right Temporal Lobe Syndrome?" *Journal of Neural Engineering* 7, no. 6 (2010): 066005; A. P. Georgopoulos, et al., "The Synchronous Neural Interactions Test as a

Functional Neuromarker for Posttraumatic Stress Disorder (PTSD): A Robust Classification Method Based on the Bootstrap," *Journal of Neural Engineering* 7. no. 1 (2010): 016011.

10. As measured on the Clinician Administered PTSD Scale (CAPS).

11. As measured by John Briere's Inventory of Altered Self-Capacities (IASC).

12. Posterior and central alpha rhythms are generated by thalamocortical networks; beta rhythms appear to be generated by local cortical networks; and the frontal midline theta rhythm (the only healthy theta rhythm in the human brain) is hypothetically generated by the septohippocampal neuronal network. For a recent review see J. Kropotov, *Quantitative EEG, ERP's And Neurotherapy* (Amsterdam: Elsevier, 2009).

13. H. Benson, "The Relaxation Response: Its Subjective and Objective Historical Precedents and Physiology," *Trends in Neurosciences* 6 *(1983)*: 281–84.

14. Tobias Egner and John H. Gruzelier, "Ecological Validity of Neurofeedback: Modulation of Slow Wave EEG Enhances Musical Performance," *Neuroreport* 14 no. 9 (2003): 1221–4; David J. Vernon, "Can Neurofeedback Training Enhance Performance? An Evaluation of the Evidence with Implications for Future Research," *Applied Psychophysiology and Biofeedback* 30, no. 4 (2005): 347–64.

15. "Vancouver Canucks Race to the Stanley Cup—Is It All in Their Minds?" Bio-Medical.com, June 2, 2011, http://bio-medical.com/news/2011/06/vancouver-canucks-race-to-the-stanley-cup-is-it-all-in-their-minds/.

16. M. Beauregard, *Brain Wars* (New York: Harper Collins, 2013), p. 33.

17. J. Gruzelier, T. Egner, and D. Vernon, "Validating the Efficacy of Neurofeedback for Optimising Performance," *Progress in Brain Research* 159 *(2006)*: 421–31. See also D. Vernon and J. Gruzelier, "Electroencephalographic Biofeedback as a Mechanism to Alter Mood, Creativity and Artistic Performance," in *Mind-Body and Relaxation Research Focus*, ed. B. N. De Luca *(*New York: Nova Science, *2008)*, 149–64.

18. See, e.g., M. Arns, et al., "Efficacy of Neurofeedback Treatment in ADHD: The Effects on Inattention, Impulsivity and Hyperactivity: A Meta-Analysis," *Clinical EEG and Neuroscience* 40, no. 3 (2009): 180–89; T. Rossiter, "The Effectiveness of Neurofeedback and Stimulant Drugs in Treating AD/HD: Part I: Review of Methodological Issues," *Applied Psychophysiology and Biofeedback* 29, no. 2 (June 2004): 95–112; T. Rossiter, "The Effectiveness of Neurofeedback and Stimulant Drugs in Treating AD/HD: Part II: Replication," *Applied Psychophysiology and Biofeedback* 29, no. 4 (2004): 233–43; and L. M. Hirshberg, S. Chiu, and J. A. Frazier, "Emerging Brain-Based Interventions for Children and Adolescents: Overview and Clinical Perspective," *Child and Adolescent Psychiatric Clinics of North America* 14, no. 1 (2005): 1–19.

19. For more on qEEG, see http://thebrainlabs.com/qeeg.shtml.

20. N. N. Boutros, M. Torello, and T. H. McGlashan, "Electrophysiological Aberrations in Borderline Personality Disorder: State of the Evidence," *Journal of Neuropsychiatry and Clinical Neurosciences* 15 (2003): 145–54.

21. In chapter 17, we saw how essential it is to cultivate a state of steady, calm self-observation, which IFS calls a state of "being in self." Dick Schwartz claims that with persistence anybody can achieve such a state, and indeed, I have seen him help very traumatized people do precisely that. I am not that skilled, and many of my most severely traumatized patients become frantic or spaced out when we approach upsetting subjects. Others feel so chronically out of control that it is difficult to find any abiding sense of "self." In most psychiatric settings people with these problems are given medications to stabilize them. Sometimes that works, but many patients lose their motivation and drive. In our randomized controlled study of neurofeedback, chronically traumatized patients had an approximately 30 percent reduction in PTSD symptoms and a significant improvement in measures of executive function and emotional control (van der Kolk et al., submitted 2014).

22. Traumatized kids with sensory-integration deficits need programs specifically developed for their needs. At present, the leaders of this effort are my Trauma Center colleague Elizabeth Warner and

Adele Diamond at the University of British Columbia.

23. R. J. Castillo, "Culture, Trance, and the Mind-Brain," *Anthropology of Consciousness* 6, no. 1 (March 1995): 17–34. See also B. Inglis, *Trance: A Natural History of Altered States of Mind* (London: Paladin, 1990); N. F. Graffin, W. J. Ray, and R. Lundy, "EEG Concomitants of Hypnosis and Hypnotic Susceptibility," *Journal of Abnormal Psychology* 104, no. 1 (1995): 123–31; D. L. Schacter, "EEG Theta Waves and Psychological Phenomena: A Review and Analysis," *Biological Psychology* 5, no. 1 (1977): 47–82; and M. E. Sabourin, et al., "EEG Correlates of Hypnotic Susceptibility and Hypnotic Trance: Spectral Analysis and Coherence," *International Journal of Psychophysiology* 10, no. 2 (1990): 125–42.

24. E. G. Peniston and P. J. Kulkosky, "Alpha-Theta Brainwave NeuroFeedback Therapy for Vietnam Veterans with Combat-Related Posttraumatic Stress Disorder," *Medical Psychotherapy* 4 (1991): 47–60.

25. T. M. Sokhadze, R. L. Cannon, and D. L. Trudeau, "EEG Biofeedback as a Treatment for Substance Use Disorders: Review, Rating of Efficacy and Recommendations for Further Research," *Journal of Neurotherapy* 12, no. 1 (2008): 5–43.

26. R. C. Kessler, "Posttraumatic Stress Disorder: The Burden to the Individual and to Society," *Journal of Clinical Psychiatry* 61, suppl. 5 (2000): 4–14. See also R. Acierno, et al., "Risk Factors for Rape, Physical Assault, and Posttraumatic Stress Disorder in Women: Examination of Differential Multivariate Relationships," *Journal of Anxiety Disorders* 13, no. 6 (1999): 541–63; and H. D. Chilcoat and N. Breslau, "Investigations of Causal Pathways Between PTSD and Drug Use Disorders," *Addictive Behaviors* 23, no. 6 (1998): 827–40.

27. S. L. Fahrion et al., "Alterations in EEG Amplitude, Personality Factors, and Brain Electrical Mapping After Alpha-Theta Brainwave Training: A Controlled Case Study of an Alcoholic in Recovery," *Alcoholism: Clinical and Experimental Research* 16, no. 3 (June 1992): 547–52; R. J. Goldberg, J. C. Greenwood, and Z. Taintor, "Alpha Conditioning as an Adjunct Treatment for Drug Dependence: Part 1," *International Journal of Addiction* 11, no. 6 (1976): 1085–89; R. F. Kaplan, et al., "Power and Coherence Analysis of the EEG in Hospitalized Alcoholics and Nonalcoholic Controls," *Journal of Studies on Alcohol* 46 (1985): 122–27; Y. Lamontagne et al., "Alpha and EMG Feedback Training in the Prevention of Drug Abuse: A Controlled Study," *Canadian Psychiatric Association Journal* 22, no. 6 (October 1977): 301–10; Saxby and E. G. Peniston, "Alpha-Theta Brainwave Neurofeedback Training: An Effective Treatment for Male and Female Alcoholics with Depressive Symptoms," *Journal of Clinical Psychology* 51, no. 5 (1995): 685–93; W. C. Scott, et al., "Effects of an EEG Biofeedback Protocol on a Mixed Substance Abusing Population," *American Journal Drug and Alcohol Abuse* 31, no. 3 (2005): 455–69; and D. L. Trudeau, "Applicability of Brain Wave Biofeedback to Substance Use Disorder in Adolescents," *Child & Adolescent Psychiatric Clinics of North America* 14, no. 1 (January 2005): 125–36.

28. E. G. Peniston, "EMG Biofeedback-Assisted Desensitization Treatment for Vietnam Combat Veterans Posttraumatic Stress Disorder," *Clinical Biofeedback and Health* 9 (1986): 35–41.

29. Eugene G. Peniston, and Paul J. Kulkosky. "Alpha-Theta Brainwave Neurofeedback for Vietnam Veterans with Combat-Related PostTraumatic Stress Disorder." *Medical Psychotherapy* 4, no. 1 (1991): 47-60.

30. Similar results were reported by another group seven years later: W. C. Scott, et al., "Effects of an EEG Biofeedback Protocol on a Mixed Substance Abusing Population," *American Journal of Drug and Alcohol Abuse* 31, no. 3 (2005): 455–69.

31. D. L. Trudeau, T. M. Sokhadze, and R. L. Cannon, "Neurofeedback in Alcohol and Drug Dependency," in Introduction to *Quantitative EEG and Neurofeedback: Advanced Theory and Applications*, ed. T. Budzynski, *et al.* Amsterdam, Elsevier, (1999) pp. 241–68; F. D. Arani, R. Rostami, and M. Nostratabadi, "Effectiveness of Neurofeedback Training as a Treatment for Opioid-Dependent Patients," *Clinical EEG and Neuroscience* 41, no. 3 (2010): 170–77; F. Dehghani-Arani, R. Rostami, and H. Nadali, "Neurofeedback Training for Opiate Addiction: Improvement of Mental

Health and Craving," *Applied Psychophysiology and Biofeedback*, 38, no. 2 (2013): 133–41; J. Luigjes, et al., "Neuromodulation as an Intervention for Addiction: Overview and Future Prospects," *Tijdschrift voor psychiatrie* 55, no. 11 (2012): 841–52.

32. S. Othmer, "Remediating PTSD with Neurofeedback," October 11, 2011, http://hannokirk.com/files/Remediating-PTSD_10-01-11.pdf.

33. F. H. Duffy, "The State of EEG Biofeedback Therapy (EEG Operant Conditioning) in 2000: An Editor's Opinion," an editorial in *Clinical Electroencephalography* 31, no. 1 (2000): v–viii.

34. Thomas R. Insel, "Faulty Circuits," *Scientific American* 302, no. 4 (2010): 44-51.

35. T. Insel, "Transforming Diagnosis," National Insitute of Mental Health, Director's Blog, April 29, 2013, http://www.nimh.nih.gov/about/director/2013/transforming-diagnosis.shtml.

36. Joshua W. Buckholtz and Andreas Meyer-Lindenberg, "Psychopathology and the Human Connectome: Toward a Transdiagnostic Model of Risk For Mental Illness," *Neuron* 74, no. 4 (2012): 990–1004.

37. F. Collins, "The Symphony Inside Your Brain," NIH Director's Blog, November 5, 2012, http://directorsblog.nih.gov/2012/11/05/the-symphony-inside-your-brain/.

CHAPTER 20: FINDING YOUR VOICE: COMMUNAL RHYTHMS AND THEATER

1. F. Butterfield, "David Mamet Lends a Hand to Homeless Vietnam Veterans," *New York Times*, October 10, 1998. For more on the new shelter, see http://www.nechv.org/historyatnechv.html.

2. P. Healy, "The Anguish of War for Today's Soldiers, Explored by Sophocles," *New York Times*, November 11, 2009. For more on Doerries's project, see http://www.outsidethewirellc.com/projects/theater-of-war/overview.

3. Sara Krulwich, "The Theater of War," *New York Times*, November 11, 2009.

4. W. H. McNeill, *Keeping Together in Time: Dance and Drill in Human History* (Cambridge, MA: Harvard University Press, 1997).

5. Plutarch, *Lives*, vol. 1 (Digireads.com, 2009), 58.

6. M. Z. Seitz, "The Singing Revolution," *New York Times*, December 14, 2007.

7. For more on Urban Improv, see http://www.urbanimprov.org/.

8. The Trauma Center Web site, offers a full-scale downloadable curriculum for a fourth-grade Urban Improv program that can be run by teachers nationwide. http://www.traumacenter.org/initiatives/psychosocial.php.

9. For more on the Possibility Project, see http://the-possibility-project.org/.

10. For more on Shakespeare in the Courts, see http://www.shakespeare.org/education/for-youth/shakespeare-courts/.

11. C. Kisiel, et al., "Evaluation of a Theater-Based Youth Violence Prevention Program for Elementary School Children," *Journal of School Violence* 5, no. 2 (2006): 19–36.

12. The Urban Improv and Trauma Center leaders were Amie Alley, PhD, Margaret Blaustein, PhD, Toby Dewey, MA, Ron Jones, Merle Perkins, Kevin Smith, Faith Soloway, Joseph Spinazzola, PhD.

13. H. Epstein and T. Packer, *The Shakespeare & Company Actor Training Experience* (Lenox MA, Plunkett Lake Press, 2007); H. Epstein, *Tina Packer Builds a Theater* (Lenox, MA: Plunkett Lake Press, 2010).

to be continue...

Manufactured by Amazon.ca
Bolton, ON

19127957R00070